HMS VICTORY

HMS VICTORY

FIRST RATE 1765

Jonathan Eastland & Iain Ballantyne

Seaforth
PUBLISHING

Copyright © Jonathan Eastland & Iain Ballantyne 2011

First published in Great Britain in 2011 by
Seaforth Publishing,
Pen & Sword Books Ltd,
47 Church Street,
Barnsley S70 2AS

www.seaforthpublishing.com

British Library Cataloguing in Publication Data

A catalogue record for this book is available from the
British Library
ISBN 978 1 84832 094 9

Art Direction and Design by Stephen Dent
Deck Plans by Tony Garrett
Printed in China through Printworks Int. Ltd

CONTENTS

Half title: Anniversary storm. A southwesterly gale screeches through the rigging of Nelson's flagship on 21 October 2004, as dawn breaks on the 199th anniversary of the battle of Trafalgar.

Title pages: Raising the ship above the dock parapet for aesthetic reasons posed numerous engineering problems for dockyard authorities.

Above left: The current figurehead is a replica of the one that was fitted in 1795 and carried at the battle of Trafalgar. It was completed in 1989.

Following pages: Portsmouth Historic Dockyard, England where the world's oldest warship is still in service. This iconic vessel is the only example of an eighteenth-century line of battle ship, most famed for her role as Vice Admiral Horatio Nelson's flagship at the 1805 battle of Trafalgar. HMS *Victory* was permanently dry-docked here in No 2 Dock in January 1922.

AT AROUND 1:15PM ON 21 OCTOBER 1805,
Lord Nelson was pacing the Quarterdeck of HMS *Victory*
with Captain Hardy when he was mortally wounded by a
musket ball, fired by a sharpshooter from the French ship
Redoutable, with which the British fleet was engaged.
As the battle of Trafalgar raged on, he was carried below
to the Orlop deck, where, some three hours later he
died, but not before he received the news that the battle
was won. These events ensured both Nelson and HMS
Victory immortality in British naval history and are widely
known.

There is no doubt that the role of the ship has
changed somewhat since then!

HMS *Victory* is the oldest commissioned warship in the
world and is still in service within the Royal Navy. It
doesn't take 821 people to run her any more but we do
have a team of over 40 people working throughout the
year to make sure the ship stays open to the public. This
dedicated team of people help me in operating the ship
in each of her three main roles: Firstly, she is the Flagship
of the Second Sea Lord and Commander-in-Chief Naval
Home Command, Vice Admiral Charles Montgomery
CBE ADC. The Admiral often hosts formal events
onboard his Flagship, be it a VIP dinner in the Great
Cabin, or presentations of Elizabeth Crosses to widows
of servicemen killed in action. It is my responsibility to
ensure that the ship is ready in all respects for this and
that the events run smoothly.

Secondly, the ship is a world class tourist attraction.
We receive around 350,000 visitors each year and it is
important that each visitor has a good experience
onboard and gets the most out of their visit.

Thirdly, as a living museum to the Georgian navy, we
are part of a wider organisation within Portsmouth
Historic Dockyard which includes the newly formed
National Museum of the Royal Navy, *Warrior* 1860, and
the *Mary Rose*.

HMS *Victory* survived the battle of Trafalgar, she survived
a hit from a German bomb during the Second World
War and she continues to hold a unique position in the
affections of the Royal Navy and the Nation. It is a huge
privilege for me to be in command of one of the world's
greatest ships, she is a constant reminder to me of a
great period in our history. This book tells that history, it
weaves historical fact in with modern details to tell the
story of the ship. I thoroughly commend it to you.

Oscar Whild,
Lieutenant Commander Royal Navy,
Commanding Officer, HMS *Victory*.

To Mum;
Lots of Love,
'Douglas' Oscar
Whilst
Commanding
Officer
HMS VICTORY
21/10/11

1 | HMS VICTORY

TODAY'S PASSENGERS ON THE SLAB-SIDED CROSS-
Channel ferries departing or entering Portsmouth
Harbour see spread out before them the vast
panorama of what is arguably the most historic naval
base in the world. Prominent in this view is likely to be
the towering and sharply angled mainmast of a
modern *Daring* class destroyer, with the 200ft tall
masts, yards and mass of rigging of HMS *Victory* clearly
visible beyond. No greater contrast of naval technology
exists anywhere else in the world.

The stark contrast between computer-controlled,
laser-welded steel and the laboriously hand-hewn
wooden warship is further reinforced by the huge 'golf
ball' atop HMS *Daring*'s mainmast. It
contains a sophisticated air-defence
radar enabling the destroyer to

shoot down targets travelling at three times the speed
of sound, up to sixty miles away. *Victory*, on the other
hand, packed her punch with more than a hundred
rather less precise and far shorter-ranged long guns,
massive smoothbore cannon whose main function was
to batter an enemy into submission at point-blank
range; solid iron roundshot against timber, rather than
Sea Viper missiles against supersonic aircraft.

The technological, social and economic changes
packed into more than two centuries since the battle
of Trafalgar have been immense. Close to a thousand
men were needed for the efficient crewing of *Victory*;
today's *Daring* needs less than 200. Hundreds of lower-
deck sailors in Nelson's day slept in hammocks with
barely an inch to spare between them while today's
ratings have comfortable cabins with *en-suite* showers.

The first of the Type 45 destroyers, HMS *Daring*, is nudged alongside by
fussing tugs. In the background, her masts and rigging shrouded in a
cold January sea mist, the 244-year-old battle of Trafalgar First Rate
stands sentinel over a scene Vice Admiral Nelson would have welcomed.

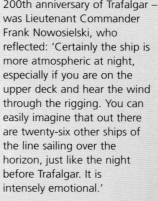

Victory's men performed their ablutions with buckets of cold water. Setting aside these and other startling contrasts, there is a great deal *Daring* and *Victory* share. The period between *Victory*'s moment of blood and thunder at the battle of Trafalgar in 1805 and *Daring*'s entry into service is not really such a long time. While form and function change, the ocean – and the exercising of sea power across the face of the planet – endures.

Today *Victory* holds the proud title of being the oldest warship still in commission in any navy, though the most elderly warship still afloat is 'Old Ironsides' – the USS *Constitution*. While *Constitution* is an impressive piece of work, and much credit is due to America for maintaining her in sailing trim, her fighting reputation as a tough-as-nails frigate lacks the epic panoply of *Victory*'s fighting life. Nor does the *Constitution* possess the same physical presence – she is a heavy frigate, not a battleship. Aboard the First Rate you tread where Nelson once fought and died. It makes any visit to the ship an almost spiritual experience. *Victory* may be permanently dry-docked, but at night, when the tourists have gone, the ghosts return. The ship's Commanding Officer in 2005 – the year of the 200th anniversary of Trafalgar – was Lieutenant Commander Frank Nowosielski, who reflected: 'Certainly the ship is more atmospheric at night, especially if you are on the upper deck and hear the wind through the rigging. You can easily imagine that out there are twenty-six other ships of the line sailing over the horizon, just like the night before Trafalgar. It is intensely emotional.'

2|THE LINE OF BATTLE

IN HER TIME, HMS *VICTORY* WAS ONE OF THE most powerful vessels afloat, a platform for 104 guns by the time she fought at Trafalgar in 1805, a truly devastating weight of firepower. As such, throughout her long career, *Victory* was a strategic tool, wielded by Britain to ensure it could carve out a place in the world with certainty and security.

The first *Victory* in English naval history was an Elizabethan race-built galleon, taken up from trade and rebuilt into a nimble warship with a single gun deck for most of her principal armament of forty-two guns. The tactics deployed by the English at the battle of the Armada (1588), in which she fought, were hit and run, with only loosely co-ordinated forays against the

Spanish fleet, nipping at its heels, pouncing on those unfortunate vessels that fell behind. Subsequent warships named *Victory* – and there have been seven in total since the sixteenth century – were more substantial weapons platforms and deployed for battle in different style. Hit-and-run fighting suited the buccaneering ways of Elizabethan seadogs, but for future foes a different form of maritime combat would be needed.

SOVEREIGN OF HER SEAS

Elizabethan warships had been nimble enough to have a significant proportion of their guns pointing forward and astern, to chase their prey and fire on them as well as to shoot at pursuers, but they were replaced by

bigger, heavier ships mounting batteries of guns on multiple decks. This made them slower, less manoeuvrable and they needed to present their broadest side to attack an enemy (hence the term for a full salvo of naval firepower being a 'broadside').

The era of the second *Victory* in the 1650s saw the advent of the line of battle, in which the destructive power of a fleet was concentrated to overcome the fact that even the biggest gun was short-ranged and accuracy was limited. Arranging the most powerful ships of a fleet in a line also offered protection astern and ahead – the vulnerable zones of a sailing warship.

The line of battle was ideally suited to the relatively slow pace of the Age of Sail, subject as it was to the vagaries of wind and tide and only elementary means of communication.

The first formal use of the line of battle is said to have been in June 1653, at the battle of Gabbard against the Dutch, at which second *Victory* fought. Not a single ship was lost on the English side; such was the skill with which General-at-Sea Robert Blake deployed the new line of battle. In consultation with other senior Generals-at-Sea, he had formulated the famous *Fighting Instructions*, which made it clear that as soon

The battle of Quiberon Bay. Outstanding British seamanship was a factor that encouraged Hawke to bring the French fleet to action on a dark afternoon in November 1759 when, in a raging sea and rising westerly gale, he closed with one of the most dangerous lee shores in Europe and drove the French into Quiberon Bay. This victory freed England from the threat of invasion and the naming of *Victory* in the same year was a sign of the Royal Navy's mastery of the seas. (© *National Maritime Museum, Greenwich*)

as it seemed a fleet engagement was imminent, squadrons should bring their ships into line with the fleet commander's, imposing the tactical formation of line ahead. It is likely the line of battle had been used before by one or more of the Generals-at-Sea, but the *Fighting Instructions* set the seal upon it and in the reign of King Charles II the doctrine was formalised into a handbook for senior officers. The rank of Admiral replaced that of General-at-Sea, while seniority depended on which squadron an officer commanded in the line of battle. The most senior was the Admiral of the Red Squadron, in the centre, followed by the Admiral of the White Squadron, at the head of the line, and then Admiral of the Blue Squadron, at the rear. To denote which squadron a ship belonged to, she flew an appropriate ensign, for the standardisation on the White Ensign for all British warships did not occur until the 1860s.

SHIPS OF THE LINE

By the late eighteenth century, the 100-gun ship was the ultimate expression of naval power, though warships of 74 guns and upward were considered strong enough to take their place in the line of battle. The terms 'battleship' and 'ship of the line' were born. Warships were also classified by 'rates': First Rate (100 guns or more, three gun decks), Second Rate (90 guns or more, similarly with three gun decks) and Third Rate (74 guns, two gun decks). All of these were line of battle ships. Fourth Rates (50 guns, two gun decks), Fifth Rates and Sixth Rates (36–24 guns, one gun deck) were collectively known as 'cruisers', or frigates. Because of their size, First Rates were ideally suited to the job of flagship, so, wherever she served, the *Victory* of Nelson's era could expect to be in the thick of the action.

An admiral pacing the poop deck of a First Rate gained a commanding view of his entire fleet and *Victory* was blessed with fine sailing qualities matching her powerful armament, making her one of the swiftest and deadliest ships afloat. In the line of battle the admiral placed his ship near the centre of the line of battle, in the aforementioned Red Squadron, so flag signals could be seen – hence the admiral's ship being known as the 'flagship'. Only the ships immediately ahead and behind the admiral in the line of battle could instantly and clearly see his instructions, however, so they would be transmitted up and down the line by successive ships flying the same signal flags, or even relayed by a frigate standing off on the disengaged side of the line during a battle, well out of the smoke.

In a sea fight, the impact of variables often took its toll before battle could be joined. The costly, gentle-manly process of assembling the line might begin in the morning, but be so drawn out that by the time it was complete night might have fallen. Perhaps, with darkness closing in rapidly during autumn or winter, engaging the enemy might be impossible. The weather might also change dramatically, scattering ships or making it difficult for them to join up in the first place. Then there was the potentially restrictive nature of the *Fighting Instructions* themselves, always subject to modification by each major fleet commander as the needs of the moment demanded, but which, if followed to the letter, could lead to a lack of initiative in individual captains. They might always be looking to follow the leader, out of fear perhaps, or just lack of aggression.

The difference between victory and defeat might come down to the finer points. National character, economic and strategic priorities as well as seamanship and gunnery skills all came into play. The French and Spanish were not keen on getting into slugging matches and tended to aim for masts and rigging in order to disable the enemy. This would enable them to escape the fearsome gunnery of Royal Navy warships, which would be concentrated on the hulls of their opponents to batter them into submission.

The British staked almost everything on their navy and due to seamanship, tactics, the genius of commanders, and the stout 'hearts of oak' of the ordi-nary sailors, they won most of the time, forging the so-called 'habit of Victory'. There were exceptions. Among them, in the Royal Navy's case, the conduct of British commander Rear Admiral Thomas Graves at the battle of Chesapeake in 1781, embarked aboard his flagship HMS *London*, a 98-gun Second Rate built at Chatham and launched a year after *Victory*. Graves adhered to the letter of the *Fighting Instructions*, spending too much time arranging his line of battle. His cautious conduct of a line-of-battle clash and subsequent withdrawal for his ships to effect repairs allowed a French supply convoy to slip into Chesapeake Bay and land both troops and siege guns, enabling the American rebels to force the British to surrender at Yorktown.

However, there was a revolution in naval warfare brewing, though, and a series of battles, some involving HMS *Victory*, would reveal to the world a new breed of British fighting captain. These men were prepared to tear through the confines of the *Fighting Instructions* and shatter the gentlemanly conduct of the line of battle. It culminated in *Victory*'s finest hour as the flagship of the foremost naval genius of the age, Horatio Nelson, at the battle of Trafalgar.

3|WITH A HEART OF OAK

A NEW FIRST RATE

In 1758, with the nation locked into a global conflict with France, there was a pressing need for a new First Rate, a survey of the fleet having discovered only the 104-gun *Royal George* fit for service. On 13 December the warship that would become the seventh *Victory* was one of a dozen major new constructions ordered, her keel eventually laid on 23 July 1759 in the Old Single Dock at Chatham Royal Dockyard. With a design by Senior Surveyor of the Navy Sir Thomas Slade, based on that of the handsome *Royal George*, the new First Rate's specification called for 100 guns carried on three gun decks. She would displace more than 2,000 tons, making her the largest warship ever built for the British fleet. Her length would be 227ft 6in – her decks were 186ft long – with a beam of 52ft while she would draw 25ft of water 'at mean load'.

The requirements set down for such a vessel could not, however, be adequately handled by the formalised dimensions laid down under the existing Establishment, which dictated the size of virtually every piece of timber utilised in the construction of a British naval vessel, if not the finer points of the design itself. The aim of an Establishment was to have uniformity across the fleet in the various rates, so their sailing qualities and fighting power would (hopefully) be standardised, enabling fleet

commanders to wield a cohesive force. In reality, ships were rebuilt throughout their careers and suffered changes in their capabilities, so the ideal was very hard to achieve. Not only that, if a design was defective in the first place (such as not being able to open lower gun ports in less than benign conditions), it would be a flaw inflicted across a number of key vessels. Action was taken by the Board of the Admiralty, with a new 1745 Establishment resetting dimensions permitted for warships under the original 1719 Establishment, which had been revised, unsuccessfully, as recently as 1741. However, even the revised dimensions set down under the 1745 Establishment proved inadequate. Further amendments were introduced, and so the future *Victory* had her length increased by some 8ft, enabling armament to be increased by four more guns.

THE FINEST WARSHIP OF HER AGE

The man who designed *Victory* has been described as the best naval architect Britain produced in the eighteenth century and she afforded Slade his first, and last, opportunity to design a First Rate. She would be renowned as the finest such ship of her age.

The new First Rate was officially named *Victory* at the end of October 1760, although even some years after the loss of the last ship of the name – Admiral

Chatham Dockyard seen from Fort Pitt, drawn by G Shepherd and engraved by R Roff, 1828. *Victory* was laid down in the dockyard on 23 July 1759, left centre, and floated up on 7 May 1765.

Balchen's tragic flagship, which had disappeared with all hands in a stormy Channel in the autumn of 1744 – there was considerable hesitation about allowing it to be carried by a new vessel. However, there was no adverse reaction in the country, especially as the year the requirement was set down for a new *Victory* was arguably when Britain secured her status as the predominant global naval power, in battles from Quebec to Quiberon Bay. There had been stunning victories against the French both at sea and on land, and so the name reflected the mood of confidence in the country. Britain would need ships like the new First Rate to safeguard its gains.

A reputation for success and status as a lucky ship would secure *Victory* an unrivalled place in the affections of the admirals. Some of her contemporaries might pass from service and be sent to the breakers', but *Victory* was, for most of her career, kept in good repair and ready for action. She represented the excel-lent combination of firepower and speed. Large, fast, powerful and manoeuvrable, she had the required ability to shrug aside heavy seas and carry enough stores to range the world's oceans.

A TOUGH CUSTOMER

Victory's construction consumed 6,000 oak trees, almost a hundred acres of woodland, though not all of it was English, much being imported from the Baltic regions and Poland. Some of the timber had been stockpiled at Chatham as far back as 1746. Oak was the primary wood used in the construction of warships – the seafaring anthem *Hearts of Oak* was composed in the year *Victory*'s construction commenced – a resource taking time to mature, for it took a century for an acorn to grow to a mature tree big enough to provide timber for ship building. If Britain was unable to build enough First Rates, it could reasonably be blamed on whoever had failed to create the forests a

A contemporary model of the earlier 100-gun *Victory*, of 1737, depicts a more high-sided vessel, typical of the older generation. Her crew of 1,100 men were drowned when she was lost on the Channel Islands in 1744. (© *National Maritime Museum, Greenwich*)

One of the dockyard models, commissioned by Lord Sandwich for George III in 1771, depicts *Victory* in the dock at Chatham just before floating out, surrounded by the offices, workshops, stores and docks of an eighteenth-century dockyard. The Royal Dockyards were the largest industrial complexes of their era. *(© National Maritime Museum, Greenwich)*

century earlier. In the case of *Victory*'s generation of warships, builders were drawing on timber from oak trees theoretically planted during the reign of Oliver Cromwell.

In the 1750s and 1760s, English oak grew so scarce the British had to turn to the Baltic, but the German variety was not so strong and warships using it as a major component in their construction lasted not much more than a couple of decades. Fortunately *Victory* had enough English oak to last the distance and more. Ships built of it could last decades without a major refit and might expect to last up to a century in one form or another. Warship construction was an art; it required

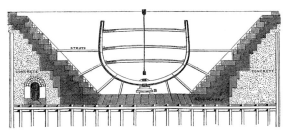

Victory's keel was laid in Chatham Dockyard's No 2 dock built in 1623, similar to the one in this nineteenth-century print.

patience to ensure the wood was properly seasoned, in order to make it resilient enough to withstand the half-century or more a major vessel could expect to be in frontline service. A decade was not uncommon, but *Victory*'s timber was subjected to the process for a further four years. Such prolonged seasoning is thought to be a major reason why the ship managed to survive so many years in service. Even today there are still some of the original timbers in her, between 10 and 15 per cent of her fabric.

By the 1750s, the Royal Navy was already the most sophisticated military-industrial enterprise on the planet with its major dockyards at Chatham, Portsmouth and Plymouth Dock, while the new *Victory* was one of man's most expensive and complex products. Once in service she would require further lengthy and expensive maintenance and huge effort to operate. According to Chatham Dockyard's records 150 men were employed creating *Victory*'s oak frame, using copper bolts 6ft long and 2in in diameter together with wooden treenails that would not corrode, to pin it all together. Another 100 workers were employed in other aspects of her construction. When it was securely assembled, *Victory*'s frame was covered, to protect it from the worst effects of the weather, and left to season further

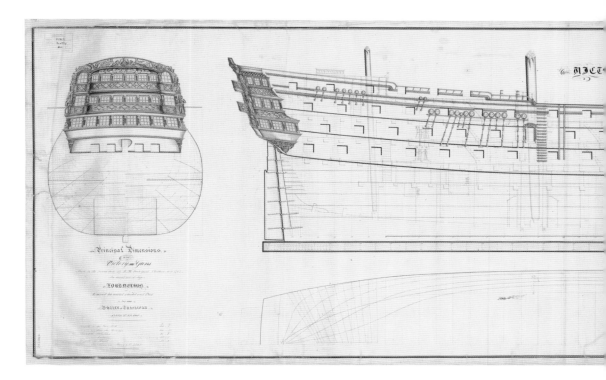

throughout much of 1760. Once she had been named on 28 October, construction continued, but slowed with the end of hostilities in 1763. The naval budget has always been tighter in times of peace, so the workforce labouring on *Victory* was cut to save money. During the six years she was in build, her massive timbers had more than sufficient time for residual sap to run out and evaporate and for the wood to settle in its new configuration in frame before planking up was complete. This added much to *Victory*'s strength as well as to her already-discussed longevity enabling us to walk her decks today. The hull of *Victory* was finally complete on 23 April 1765 – St. George's Day – the construction to that point having cost £63,176.

A MIGHTY SWORD SHEATHED

On 7 May, the next spring tide, *Victory* was floated out of the dock where she had been built – the water was let in at high tide, lifting her off blocks and other supports that held the ship securely during build.

Victory's future as an important strategic weapon was clear, for the Royal Standard flew from the mainmast, Union flag at the mizzen, Admiralty ensign at the foremast and Jack from the jackstaff. She was afloat but it was clear immediately she suffered from both a pronounced list to starboard and was down by the stern. In fact *Victory* drew 13ft 6in forward and 17ft 4in aft – when she was eventually fully ballasted, the

lower deck gun ports were less than 5ft above the water, for she sat at least 9in lower in the water than she was meant to. They would have to be kept closed in rough weather, to prevent *Victory* shipping water, but fortunately it never proved to be a serious handicap in any battle. A number of lords of the Admiralty and government ministers were there to see *Victory* afloat for the first time, as was the distinguished politician William Pitt the Elder, architect of Britain's victory in the Seven Years War. A London newspaper, the *Public Advertiser*, trumpeted in its edition of 8 May: 'Yesterday was launched at Chatham His Majesty's Ship the *Victory*, esteemed the largest and finest ship ever built.' *Victory* was not immediately fitted out to take her place on some foreign station, but rather was laid up in reserve – or Ordinary, as it was known. There was no point in exposing such a valuable vessel to the mercy of the weather on peacetime patrolling. First Rates – at the time of her launch there were only six of them in the British fleet – were the ultimate weapon, to be kept sheathed in time of peace and only drawn when really required. Warships could not just be whistled up out of thin air and fortunately the pace of technological development was such that, with judicious maintenance, repairs, and even substantial works, a warship laid up in Ordinary for some years might still be a powerful player. *Victory* suffered some leaks, which required the replacement of defective planking in March 1768, with further

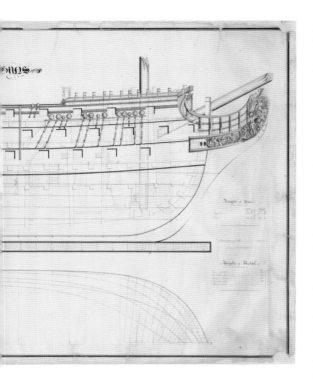

A 1:48 scale drawing of *Victory*'s body plan on the left, profile and longitudinal half-breadth. This shows how she may have looked before the great repair of 1801–03. The most prominent change was the closed stern. This drawing shows the open stern galleries, which were accessed from the Captain's and Admiral's decks. (© *National Maritime Museum, Greenwich*)

requirements. When finally completed in February 1778, *Victory* had a displacement of 3,500 tons. With her complete suite of thirty-six sails set – almost four acres of canvas – the new ship could average a healthy six knots and under the right conditions might make as much as twelve. Throughout her career, and like every other warship in the world at the time, *Victory* of course carried muzzle-loading guns. Her original weapons fit was meant to be thirty 42pdr guns, twenty-eight 24pdrs, thirty 12pdrs and a dozen 6pdrs. The number varied between 92 and 104 – the latter representing her armament at Trafalgar in 1805: thirty 32pdr guns, twenty-eight 24pdrs, forty-four 12pdrs and two 68pdr carronades. To ensure stability the heaviest guns were placed on the lower gun deck, the 24pdrs on the middle deck, and thirty of the 12pdrs on the upper gun deck, twelve on the quarter-deck and two on her forecastle deck with the carronades. The heaviest weapon *Victory* was designed to carry was the aforementioned 42pdr, a single example of which weighed in at three tons. Like all such smoothbore guns, it was classified by the weight of shot fired. However, there were two schools of thought on this formidable weapon: Admirals Samuel Hood and John Jervis, amongst others, liked the 42pdr's heavy punch, while Vice Admiral the Honourable Augustus Keppel, Commander-in-Chief, Channel Fleet, who would soon fly his flag in *Victory*, and the future Admiral Lord Nelson (by the end of 1778 captain of the sloop HMS *Badger*) preferred the 32pdr, which at 2.79 tons was easier for a gun crew to handle and could therefore achieve a higher rate of fire. The actual penetrative effect of a 32pdr round-shot was not much less than that of the more cumber-some 42pdr. Even at the long range of 1,200ft a 32pdr ball could smash its way through timbers 42in thick. This was overkill, for the fiercest parts of most fleet actions were fought with opposing warships almost touching. Furthermore, when hot from firing, the 42pdr – cast from bronze or brass – tended to recoil more violently than the iron 32pdr. In 1778, therefore, Keppel did not hesitate to order *Victory*'s 42pdrs replaced with 32pdrs. The ship's structure would not be put under as much strain while she was at sea, while less men were needed to crew them.

Within weeks of commissioning *Victory* would receive her baptism of fire.

repairs to more serious problems three years later, both instances requiring her to be docked. In the latter case *Victory* was released from her moorings in the Medway with all haste. Severe flooding occurred after boards in the bottom of her hull had sprung, the amount of water taken in raising the real prospect of her sinking. *Victory* remained in Ordinary for thirteen years until, in December 1776, the Admiralty decided it was time to bring her into service. The reason for this was the increasing likelihood of conflict with France and Spain, who were making warlike noises about supporting the American colonies in their bid for freedom. The Continental Congress had adopted the Declaration of Independence on 4 July that year, hostilities between the colonies and Britain having broken out in 1775. Mindful of the global nature of the previous major war, the British were wisely regenerating their naval power and *Victory*'s emergence from reserve was part of that process.

On being assessed suitable for service, the three-decker was put into dock for the repairs and fitting out that would make her a fully-fledged warship. While craftsmen were busy creating her sails, in the ropery at Chatham Dockyard rigging and anchor cables were spun from hemp. Meanwhile, the guns were brought aboard – they had not been installed while she was in Ordinary, to avoid unnecessary strain on *Victory*'s structure and also reduce maintenance

4 | OFF TO WAR

HMS *VICTORY*'S BAPTISM OF FIRE CAME AT THE controversial battle of Ushant in 1778, an inconclusive brush with the French in the English Channel that trailed in its wake accusations of cowardice against Vice Admiral Keppel, of which he was exonerated. In March 1780, *Victory* entered another maintenance and refit period, receiving copper sheathing on her hull below the waterline. While it increased the speed of a ship, coppering *Victory*'s bottom also prevented worms and other marine creatures from eating into her timbers. The ship received an additional six 18pdr carronades on her poop deck and two 24pdr carronades on her forecastle, while Keppel's 32pdr guns on the lower gun deck were replaced with 42pdrs.

USHANT 1781

By the middle of December 1781, the French had assembled a fleet consisting of nineteen major warships and numerous transports in Brest, in part intended for an invasion of Jamaica, Britain's richest overseas possession. Having sailed on 10 December, two days later the French spotted the masts of British warships on the horizon. The commander of the interception force was Rear Admiral Richard Kempenfelt, his flag flying in *Victory*, accompanied by eleven ships of the line, a 50-gun ship and several frigates. As his ships approached the French convoy off Ushant, on a hazy 12 December, with fog encroaching, the French admiral De Guichen fulfilled Kempenfelt's dreams of glory and prosperity by leaving such a wide gap between his warships and transports that he was unable to protect them properly. In the Age of Sail it was the ambition of any naval commander in a sea fight to win a decisive edge by gaining the weather-gage, in other words to place his warships upwind of the enemy. In that way he had freedom of manoeuvre denied to the opponent, who had to beat upwind in order to defend himself. Covered by the fog, and handling his fleet nimbly thanks to well-judged and professionally-executed flag signals, Kempenfelt was able to creep up on the French. With the weather-gage firmly in his grasp, Kempenfelt launched his force on the vulnerable merchant ships, which scattered every which way to avoid capture, for the only thing they could do – lacking the armament and fighting skill of warships – was to flee with the wind in their sails. The French warships, still ahead and to leeward, could do nothing, although four frigates tried to intervene, but were seen off by the formidable broadsides of

Kempenfelt's battleships. Fifteen vessels laden with hundreds of troops, stores and money for the West Indies were rounded up by the British and taken off to Plymouth, their loss causing great damage to the French war effort. Only two warships and five transports made it to the Caribbean, while the rest subsequently fled back to Brest after being hit by a storm.

HOWE'S DUEL AND HOOD'S FURY

Controversy was associated with *Victory* again in 1782, thanks to an unsatisfactory brush off Cape Spartel between a fleet commanded by Admiral Richard Howe with his flag in the First Rate, and the Franco-Spanish Combined Fleet. Howe had always been a fierce defender of his honour and when a fellow naval officer accused him of not leading the fleet with sufficient spirit he challenged the man to a duel. When Howe and his accuser duly met, with seconds standing by, the latter suddenly offered a grovelling apology.

By 1793, *Victory* was flagship of Admiral Samuel Hood throughout the unsatisfactory occupation of the French port of Toulon, an operation in which the Royal Navy and Spanish fleets assisted the Royalist French against the Revolutionaries. *Victory* and the rest of the Mediterranean Fleet withdrew after a young artillery officer named Napoleon Bonaparte seized the crucial Fort Mulgrave, which dominated the harbour and had been partly defended by gunners from *Victory*. Bonaparte began to fire red-hot shot at the British ships and the ill-advised adventure was abandoned. French shore batteries were soon firing at *Victory* again, this time when she dropped anchor off Corsica for another unfortunate intervention on land in 1794. Among the casualties treated by *Victory*'s ship's doctor was a young Captain Horatio Nelson, who had lost the sight in one eye while commanding naval guns ashore.

On returning to Britain aboard *Victory* to ask for more warships, Hood was outraged at not being given what he wanted. He launched furious attacks on politicians and the Admiralty and was sacked for his trouble, told to pull down his flag in *Victory*. Hood never held another sea command.

CAPE ST VINCENT

By early 1797 Britain was under serious threat from invasion and all it needed was a concentration of enemy battleships. A combined Franco-Dutch-Spanish fleet in the Channel might amount to sixty ships of the line while the most the Royal Navy might be able to assemble in British waters would be forty. The skill and

Victory painted by Monamy Swaine around 1795. She may be heading down Channel, bound for the Mediterranean in 1793, flying the flag of Lord Hood, Vice Admiral of the Red. The open stern galleries are clearly visible; these were closed in when she underwent the great repair of 1801–03. (© *National Maritime Museum, Greenwich*)

fighting quality of the Royal Navy was undoubted, but sheer weight of numbers risked overcoming that advantage.

To Admiral Sir John Jervis, commanding the Mediterranean Fleet and flying his flag in *Victory*, the primary objective was to prevent that concentration of force. Admiral Don Jose de Cordova was in command of Spain's Grand Fleet of twenty-seven ships of the line, a dozen frigates and other vessels. The Spanish were willing to attempt a breakthrough to Brest where they could combine with the Dutch and French. However, along the way they had to escort vessels conveying troops and supplies to Algeciras while providing protection for four armed merchant ships bound for Cadiz carrying mercury needed to process silver for the Franco-Spanish war effort. In his fleet Admiral Cordova had six powerful 112-gun sail of the line, a four-decker, a pair of 80s and eighteen 74s. The Spanish 112-gun ships were, on paper at least, more powerful than even *Victory*, while Cordova himself flew his flag in the massive *Santissima Trinidad*, a four-decker of 136 guns, reputed to be the largest warship in the world. She

was handicapped, however, by the poor quality of her crew, a French admiral remarking that the *Santissima Trinidad* was 'manned by herdsmen and beggars'.

In the early hours of 14 February 1797 the Spanish fleet was about thirty miles off Cape St Vincent, heading for Cadiz, a Portuguese frigate sending news to *Victory* that the enemy force was fifteen miles away. It was a dull overcast morning, with mist on the water and at 9am a lookout posted at *Victory*'s masthead reported enemy battleships. The Spanish fleet had become divided into two groups and at 11am the British commander signalled for the fleet to form line of battle. Jervis could have pounced on the smaller Spanish group but then the enemy main fleet would have the weather-gage and could easily envelop his ships. It was better to exploit the gap and then turn on the bigger group, for it would be very difficult for the smaller Spanish division to beat upwind into battle. The *Victory*'s log recorded how the enemy was sharply dealt with, the flagship herself halting the advance of a whole Spanish division: 'Raked her both ahead and astern… appeared to be in great confusion [and] bore

Nelson boarding the *San Josef* at the battle of Cape St Vincent, a favourite subject for artists of the period. *(© National Maritime Museum, Greenwich)*

up, as did six other of the enemy's ships.' According to Jervis' memoirs the Spanish battleship *Principe d'Asturias* came on until within pistol shot, but '*Victory*, sternly backing her main topsail, to look her antagonist in the face… so panic-struck the Spaniard, that he put his helm down.' The enemy discharged her starboard guns, which were elevated and so did little damage, but *Victory*'s broadsides 'so terrified him that when his sails filled, he squared his yards, ran clear out of the battle altogether, and did not return'. Meanwhile, Jervis realised the main Spanish force would cross astern to try and join up with the enemy's leeward division. However, with superb ship captains, including Nelson, under his command, who could be trusted to use their initiative rather than stick rigidly to the line of battle, the enemy was kept separated and defeated piecemeal.

On *Victory*'s poop-deck Jervis was nearly killed by a Spanish roundshot, which just missed him but smashed the head of a sailor standing nearby, *Victory*'s only fatality during the battle. The British captured four ships of the line – *Salvador del Mundo*, *San Josef*, *San Nicolas* and *San Isidro* – but more importantly the strategic goal of preventing the Spanish joining up with the French was achieved, in all a good day's work. The *Victory* had her aforementioned single fatality plus five wounded, overall casualties for the British being seventy-three killed and 227 wounded.

Jervis transferred his flag to the *Ville de Paris* and, on returning home, *Victory* was paid off at Chatham on 26 November 1797. She appeared certain only of an undignified future as a hospital ship for prisoners of war, *Victory*'s sailors and marines being scattered to the four winds. It would turn out not to be the end of her fighting life, however. In December 1799, it was ordered that *Victory* should be returned to service as a warship, following whatever repairs were needed. When commissioned back into service in 1803 – her brass 42pdr guns replaced by 32pdrs once again – she would welcome back Horatio Nelson, who would fight, and die, aboard *Victory* in the greatest sea battle in history.

5 | TRAFALGAR: THE BATTLE AND AFTER

NELSON WAS A FIRM BELIEVER IN ANNIHILATION in a sea fight, in applying decisive force to a particular point, to break through and create chaos, disrupting the orderly line of battle. He wanted to trap the enemy fleet in the chaos of multiple ship-to-ship actions at close quarters. His inspiration for this approach came not only from his own experience – at the battle of the Nile in 1798, for example, where daring and unorthodox tactics had delivered a crushing victory over the French – but also the exploits of Admiral Rodney and other predecessors who had sought the same solution. During a visit to his friend Lord Sidmouth, on 10 September 1805 – four days before he embarked in *Victory* at Portsmouth, bound for command of the Mediterranean Fleet – Nelson had explained that, should he be able to bring the Combined Fleet to battle, then he intended cutting through their line. Rodney had managed this feat at the battle of Martinique in 1780, and Nelson was

convinced it could be enlarged upon. On reaching the Mediterranean, the new flagship did not immediately take over from *Royal Sovereign*, flying the flag of Admiral Cuthbert Collingwood, a good friend of Nelson's, instead going close to Cadiz for a look at the enemy – *Victory*'s lookouts counting the masts of at least thirty-five ships of the line. Joining the fleet properly the following evening, Nelson celebrated his forty-seventh birthday on 29 September. He invited fifteen senior officers to dinner aboard the flagship, providing an opportunity to outline battle plans. Calling his doctrine 'The Nelson Touch' – an all-out aggressive assault to cut through the enemy line in more than one place to divide and conquer – he was delighted to see its impact on his officers was 'like an electric shock'. Nelson envisaged two divisions cutting the Franco-Spanish line and a third, fast division taking advantage of any enemy weakness at the decisive point. By cutting through the Franco-Spanish line ahead of, and

A drawing of Nelson's plan of attack on the Combined Fleet at Trafalgar by Gunner William Rivers. It shows French and Spanish rates and dispositions at the top, with the British fleet in two columns below. Alphanumeric codes of each ship icon identify their names.

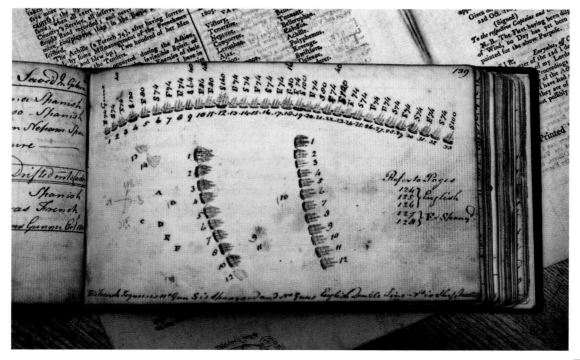

behind, the flagship of the enemy commander-in-chief, he aimed to disrupt his foe's command and control, and also achieve local superiority in numbers in the ensuing chaos and confusion, in what Nelson called a 'pell-mell' battle at close quarters. The plan would make the best of the Royal Navy's superior fighting skills to offset the disadvantage of allowing the enemy to concentrate heavy fire on the head of oncoming British ships, which would not be able to bring their broadsides to bear until the moment they cut through the line. However, they would then be able to pour fire into the exposed sterns of the enemy ships, potentially taking them out of the fight at a single stroke.

DAWN OF DESTINY

Sunrise on 21 October 1805 revealed to Nelson the keen, sharp silhouettes of the enemy, a thin mist slowly dispersing to present a beautiful morning, sea twinkling under a clear sky, a light wind from the west but a significant, long and rolling swell.

At half past six *Victory* signalled the fleet to turn east in two columns in order of sailing. Ten minutes later her flags declared: 'Prepare for battle.' With vessels absent from the British fleet, due to convoy escort work and other causes, Nelson only had enough ships of the line for two divisions – his idea for a roving third division could not be realised. No matter, for there was every chance a battle could be fought and won before nightfall and the storm threatening in the west broke. Cape Trafalgar was some twenty miles beyond the Combined Fleet, which was to leeward and now heading south.

At 9am *Victory* beat to quarters, just as she signalled the fleet to form two lines and bear down on the enemy. Nelson in *Victory* was leading the weather line, with Collingwood in *Royal Sovereign* the lee (or more southerly) one. There were eleven battleships following *Victory*, with the 64-gun *Africa* coming down from the north to join the battle, and thirteen behind *Royal Sovereign*, all managing, at most, only three knots – walking pace. Contemplating the enemy fleet strung out before him, Nelson signalled Collingwood: 'I intend to pass through the van of the enemy's line, to prevent him from getting into Cadiz.' It would be impossible for Nelson to exert any control once *Victory* was among the enemy ships but he had foreseen all this and had therefore issued a memorandum on his plan of attack. The captains would all know what to do without further orders.

At 11.40am, Nelson approached *Victory*'s Lieutenant of Signals, John Pasco, advising him: ' I wish to say to the fleet, "England confides that every man will do his duty." You must be quick, for I have one more signal to make which is for close action.' Lieutenant Pasco explained 'expects' might be better than 'confides' as the latter would have to be spelt out letter by letter. Nelson assented: 'That will do, Pasco, make it directly.'

So, up it ran, a signal that has become the most famous in naval history, as well as one of the most used, and abused, phrases in the English language.

'England expects that every man will do his duty.'

Shortly after *Victory* hoisted Nelson's last general signal to the fleet: 'Engage the enemy more closely.'

Cuthbert Collingwood was putting it into practice already, *Royal Sovereign* crashing into the enemy after

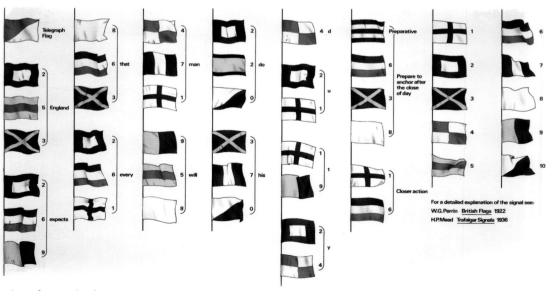

Nelson's famous signal.

enduring a terrible storm of shot, provoking Nelson to exclaim as he looked on in admiration: 'See how that noble fellow Collingwood takes his ship into action.'

With the first shots from the enemy, all British ships had broken out White Ensigns. Normally, of course, they would fly white, blue or red ensigns depending on the rank of their admirals and their position in the line of battle but, in order to avoid confusion with similar flags on enemy ships, Nelson had ordered all of his should fly the White Ensign.

Fulfilling the function of the missing third division, *Victory* was intent on carrying out a feint, closely followed by *Temeraire*, making a lunge for the enemy's van, in order to prevent them from doubling around to assist the rest of the Combined Fleet. It also had the benefit of making the French commander Admiral Villeneuve's centre division hurry forward, leaving the Franco-Spanish rear gravely outnumbered and at Collingwood's mercy. Once Nelson saw his feint had succeeded, he ordered *Victory* to make a turn to starboard, running down the enemy line, searching for the French flagship, *Bucentaure*. He found her astern of the Spanish flagship *Santissima Trinidad*, a tempting gap between the two vessels, ideal for *Victory* to cut through. Villeneuve ordered *Bucentaure* to close the gap ahead, between her and *Santissima Trinidad*, forcing *Victory* to pass astern of the French flagship. The British First Rate endured the lethal attentions of the enemy, her speed slowing to a crawling pace, yet on board, in the eye of the storm, there was an astonishing calm. A shot shattered *Victory*'s wheel, remarkably not killing any of the sailors manning it, but forcing the Master, Thomas Atkinson, and the First Lieutenant, John Quillam, to dash below, where they rigged up auxiliary steering. *Victory* was momentarily out of control, but Atkinson soon had her back in hand, with help from forty seamen. Hardy and Nelson had their own close shave when a roundshot tore through some hammocks, hit a boat and passed between them. They paused to check each other over, noticing a wood splinter had taken the buckle off one of Hardy's shoes, bruising his foot, but neither man was otherwise injured.

... BUT STILL SHE CAME ON

Victory endured forty minutes in which she could not bring her firepower to bear, for she was for the most part bows-on to the enemy. Twenty men were killed and thirty wounded and Nelson was much impressed by the crew's stoicism, telling Hardy he had never seen anything like it.

Victory's mizzen topmast was knocked down, fore topmast and maintop gallant gone, studding sails shot away, but still she came on, her deck forward a complete tangle of rigging, spars and shattered masts. The enemy was meanwhile trying to close gaps in their line, to prevent the British breaking through, Hardy remarking that it looked 'closed like a forest'. *Victory*'s captain chose the *Redoubtable*, astern of the flagship, as his target, because she was smaller than *Bucentaure* and this had the added advantage of opening the latter up to devastating raking fire. To Captain Jean-Jacques Lucas in *Redoubtable* the *Victory* looked unstoppable, so close to the French flagship's stern her yardarms passed over the other vessel's poop deck.

When the moment of truth came, *Victory* was able to pour devastating fire in from every angle, her 68pdr carronade hurling a massive roundshot and a keg containing 500 musket balls through *Bucentaure*'s stern windows. In quick succession her larboard broadside guns spat solid shot, while cannons on the quarterdeck and upper gun deck sprayed grape. Dust disturbed by the shattering of *Bucentaure*'s stern settled on the uniforms of *Victory*'s officers. Gunners in the First Rate listened with satisfaction to the crash of their shot carving a path of destruction from one end of the enemy ship to the other. The *Bucentaure* ceased to be an effective fighting vessel, with scores of dead and wounded and many of her guns dismounted. The impact of such raking fire was truly horrific, creating a scene that defied the imagination. One shot had ricocheted around the gun deck, killing or wounding at least forty men. All her masts were brought down.

The French *Neptune* raked *Victory* from ahead as the British ship crashed into *Redoubtable*. The gunners in both ships now applied themselves whole-heartedly to their grim task and, as French grapeshot swept *Victory*'s upper decks, Lieutenant Pasco was one of those badly wounded. The flagship's ordeal by fire had only just begun, the fight descending into the 'pell-mell battle' Nelson had sought. It was unfortunate that *Victory* found herself locked in a fight to the death with a French warship whose crew had trained ceaselessly for just such an eventuality. *Redoubtable*'s men had endlessly rehearsed sharp-shooting skills, grenade throwing and boarding techniques. Lucas knew his vessel could not cope with the firepower of a large British ship, nor the sheer rate of fire. Therefore, he decided to close the lower gun ports and bring the majority of his men on to the upper deck, in order to create a storm of small arms fire and grenades, hopefully clearing *Victory*'s decks for a mass boarding, grappling hooks holding the enemy vessel fast. There were even small mortars in *Redoubtable*'s fore and main tops. Seeing *Redoubtable*'s lower gunports close, and thinking the French ship had struck, *Victory*'s gunners paused but soon returned to their labours. The hellish maelstrom regained its savage intensity.

'FIRE AWAY AS FAST AS YOU CAN'

Staring at the carnage around him on the poop deck, Lieutenant Lewis Roteley of the Royal Marines felt it had become 'a slaughterhouse' with twenty marines already dead or wounded. French soldiers in the tops, barely forty-five feet away, were picking off British officers and men while repeated attempts were being made to clamber aboard. To repel them Captain Charles Adair, commander of Victory's marine detachment, had only ten men left. Adair, who had been wounded in the forehead by splinters, sent Roteley down below to bring up marines manning the guns. Despite his wound Adair raised a musket and, taking aim, shouted to Roteley as he returned with reinforcements: 'Fire away as fast as you can.' Within seconds a musket ball hit Adair in the back of the neck, killing him instantly.

On seeing the Royal Marine officer's corpse being carried away, Nelson remarked: 'There goes poor Adair, I may be next to follow him.' Calmly walking back and forth on the quarterdeck between the shattered wheel and the ladderway down to the Great Cabin, Nelson and Captain Hardy were the epitome of traditional British cool in the face of enemy fire. At 1.15pm, however, one step short of his usual turning point,

Thomas Luny's depiction of the battle of Trafalgar after Nelson had been fatally wounded, showing *Victory* alongside the French 74-gun ship *Redoutable*; laying along her starboard side is the English *Temeraire* and beyond her the French *Fougueux*. These four great ships lay abreast each other without steerage way, unable to influence the closing stages of the battle. *(The Royal Naval Museum, Portsmouth)*

Nelson span around. Hardy turned to find the admiral on his knees, left hand on the deck in a slippery slick of blood. Suddenly, the admiral's arm gave way and he collapsed, rolling onto his left side. Fearing the worst, Hardy rushed over, enquiring with dread: 'I trust that your Lordship is not severely wounded?'

The admiral gasped: 'They have done for me at last, Hardy… My backbone is shot through.' Hardy ordered Sergeant Secker of the Royal Marines and two sailors to lift Nelson up and carry him below decks. A French soldier firing from the *Redoubtable*'s mizzen top had delivered the fatal blow. Ironically, *Victory* had no marines in her tops to counter the enemy's sharp-shooters, as Nelson forbade it, on account of the danger posed by musket fire setting his flagship's sails ablaze. As it was the enemy fighting tops were soon cleared by sailors and marines firing up from *Victory*'s decks. Whoever shot Nelson was soon killed himself. Meanwhile, other sailors and soldiers aboard *Redoubtable*'s were massing on her upper deck, ready to clamber across and take the British flagship. As they made their bid, a horde of *Victory*'s gunners rushed up from below decks, firing pistols and muskets, wielding axes, mallets and cutlasses and attacked the intruders. Five Frenchmen were the first, and last, boarders ever to set foot on *Victory*, all being killed. The French still managed to inflict further casualties by hurling down grenades and via their storm of musketry. Frustrated at being repelled, many of *Redoubtable*'s gunners raced back down to their weapons, put them on maximum elevation and began blasting roundshot up through *Victory*'s quarterdeck, sending lethal splinters flying in all directions.

In the charnel house that was *Victory*'s cockpit, the surgeon, Dr William Beatty, and his assistants continued their desperate work to save lives. To his horror the surgeon had spotted Nelson himself being brought below and with the help of others took the admiral to a midshipman's berth. On being informed he was being tended to by the surgeon, the admiral responded, fighting for breath: 'Ah, Mr Beatty… you can do nothing for me… I have… but a short time… to live… my back is shot through.' Anxious not to cause the admiral any more pain than was necessary, Beatty decided not to probe too much. There was no exit wound, but the surgeon was certain from the symptoms – rhythmic gushing of the blood inside Nelson's chest, no sensation in the lower part of the body, difficulty breathing and severe pain in the spine – that the wound was fatal, as the admiral claimed.

The battle had by now turned decisively in favour of the British, with ship after ship in the Combined Fleet striking its colours and surrendering. Although still locked in a death embrace, *Victory* and *Redoubtable*

retained forward momentum, straying into the path of *Temeraire*, which was virtually immobile due to losing her sails but eager to dish out punishment. When the *Redoubtable* came within range, *Temeraire* let rip with a devastating broadside. Soon *Redoubtable* had no guns capable of being fired and out of her 643-strong complement 522 were either dead or wounded. With *Temeraire* entering the fight on the other side, junior officers in charge of *Victory*'s starboard guns, in the middle and lower decks, ordered their weapons depressed and less powerful charges used, preventing shot from passing through *Redoubtable* and into *Temeraire*. The French vessel's mainmast came down, her rudder was shot away and there were gaping holes in her hull and decks. She had burst into flames more than once. Her end was near.

TRIUMPH AND TRAGEDY

Below decks, in *Victory*'s cockpit, the life of the great hero was ebbing away. Troubled by the sound and vibration of the *Victory*'s guns firing, Nelson could now hear loud cheering. He asked the reason for it and Lieutenant Pasco, lying wounded nearby, told the admiral enemy ships were surrendering.

However, the Combined Fleet's van squadron finally came into the battle, although ineffectually, *Victory* letting rip with her larboard guns at a French ship of the line, making to rake HMS *Colossus*. The vibration of the guns vexed the dying admiral below, making him cry out pathetically: 'Oh, *Victory*! *Victory*! How you distract my poor brain!'

Captain Hardy took the admiral's hand, hearing the greatest naval hero of the age declare he knew he had just minutes to live. Nelson was worried his corpse might be cast over the side and pleaded: 'Don't throw me overboard…'

Horrified by the very idea, Hardy replied: 'Certainly not.'

Having asked Hardy to make sure he took care of Lady Hamilton, the rapidly fading Nelson, now on the brink of delirium, asked: 'Kiss me Hardy.'

Kissing Nelson's cheek, Hardy understood that, as life seeped out of him, his old friend merely wanted some small comfort, as might a child frightened of the dark. It seemed to calm Nelson, to set him a little bit more at ease.

'Now I am satisfied,' the admiral gasped. 'Thank God, I have done my duty.'

Hardy straightened up and stood over Nelson for a little while, then, overcome with sadness, stooped down and kissed Nelson's forehead, a tender farewell.

'Who is that?' the admiral wheezed.

'It is Hardy.'

'God bless you…'

This portrait of Nelson, shown in the cockpit on *Victory* as he lay dying, was painted from a posthumous sketch of the body made by the artist Arthur William Devis when *Victory* returned to England carrying the body of the Admiral. Devis also sketched and incorporated the portraits of those who were present at the death. (© *National Maritime Museum, Greenwich*)

As he slipped away Nelson repeatedly murmured, 'Thank God, I have done my duty.' Quarter of an hour after Hardy's second kiss, Nelson lost the power of speech, becoming very feeble. The admiral hovered between life and death. When Dr Beatty returned from attending to the wounded he found Nelson's hand cold and no pulse in the wrist. Placing his own hand on Nelson's forehead, the surgeon discovered it was also ice cold. The admiral's eyes flickered momentarily. Beatty again went back to tend the wounded but was called over five minutes later to find Nelson had finally passed away. It was 4.30pm, almost the exact moment when firing ceased. Atkinson noted in the *Victory*'s log that 'a victory having been reported to the Right Honourable Lord Viscount Nelson, he then died of his wound'.

THE BALTIC

Victory herself would serve in one more theatre of war, but never engage in another major sea fight. In March 1808, Vice Admiral Sir James Saumarez – one of Nelson's 'Band of Brothers', the captains who had fought under him – hoisted his flag in *Victory*, bound for a mission to Baltic waters that would call more for diplomacy than straight at 'em aggression. The principal aim of the British deployment was to protect merchant ships, which would be escorted in convoys often several hundred vessels strong. Equally pressing was the need to counter Russian maritime power, attack enemy shipping wherever the opportunity arose, and blockade the ports of Germany, Poland and Prussia. There were two adventures beyond the Baltic

for *Victory* during this period. In mid-January 1809 she was off Corunna, to help evacuate a small British army following the defeat of both Spanish and Portuguese armies by Napoleon. The First Rate would return to Iberian waters in March 1811, dropping anchor on the Tagus to land troops reinforcing Wellington's army.

Victory left Spithead on 17 April 1812, on what would be her final Baltic deployment and, indeed, her last ever as a front-line warship. To encourage Prussia to abandon Napoleon, Saumarez agreed to desist from active operations against its shipping and even offered some measure of protection. On 24 June Napoleon unleashed his 700,000-strong *Grande Armée* against Russia, news of which was conveyed by Vice Admiral Saumarez in an immediate dispatch back to London.

The Royal Navy's warships now made their main aim the prevention of supplies getting through to feed Napoleon's armies as they marched ever deeper into Russia. In this enterprise they succeeded, for while a few enemy ships evaded the British, they were not enough to save Napoleon from disaster.

To some, *Victory*'s fighting life may appear to have ended in a whimper rather than a roar, but this would fail to understand the exercise of sea power, via capital ships whose influence extended far beyond the range of their guns. The closure of the Baltic to French supply ships had helped to ensure the destruction of both Napoleon's army and his empire. It was a triumph every bit as significant as Trafalgar, but of course without the same bloodshed.

A CURTAIN FALLS

On 28 October 1812, *Victory* weighed anchor and departed Wingo Sound for the last time, concluding her glorious fighting career. At Portsmouth, towards the end of November 1812, she was paid off into Ordinary. It was fifty-three years and four months since her keel had been laid and there were plenty of younger warships to fight Britain's battles now. There was trouble across the Atlantic, with a new war against the United States, but it was unlikely to need *Victory*. On 17 December *Victory*'s log noted: 'People employed cleaning the Ship. Drafted the ship's company to the Royal William.' With her sailors and marines living aboard the accommodation ship *Royal William*, all that remained was to return some stores to the depot and on 18 December came the final entry of *Victory*'s sea-going life: 'Moderate breezes and Snowy weather. Employed returning the remaining stores to the Victualling Office and Dock Yard etc.' And so the curtain came down, with only a half-dozen caretaker standing officers left aboard. *Victory* would sail no more off to war, but despite the odds against her survival she would remain the nation's flagship.

6|THE IMMORTAL SHIP

AFTER HER FIGHTING CAREER ENDED IN 1812
Victory narrowly escaped the fate of many historically less important ships. It was fortunate that her former captain, Thomas Hardy, became First Sea Lord for legend has it that he saved her. It is said that after signing an order to break up *Victory* in 1831 he confessed to his wife that he had done a terrible thing. She urged him to rip the order up, which he is alleged to have done the next day. In 1841 the rumour spread in the streets of London and newspapers of the major naval ports of Plymouth and Portsmouth that *Victory* was again destined for the breaker's yard. A public outcry followed and both the Admiralty and politicians noted the mood. An announcement was duly made that *Victory* would remain flagship of the Admiral Commander-in-Chief, Portsmouth, as she had been since 1825. When not used as a flagship or for training boy sailors, *Victory* was placed in Ordinary, rigged with her just lower masts, a cut-down rig and manned by a small crew, all the while hooked up to buoys in Portsmouth Harbour. A familiar sight to trippers and

Portsmouth Harbour in an early nineteenth-century engraving by W Finden after a painting by E W Cooke shows a frigate (left) being rigged ready for a commission. A Blue Ensign flies from the rigging hulk. *Victory* is seen in the middle right distance when she was probably the Port Admiral's flagship.

harbour commuters for more than 100 years, even the relative protection of one of the world's finest natural harbours could not prevent the slow but inexorable deterioration of *Victory's* fabric. Prevailing south-westerly winds and miserly peacetime army and navy budgets hastened the process; but it was an accident that almost sent her to the bottom.

In October 1903, two days after the ninety-eighth anniversary of Trafalgar, HMS *Neptune*, a 9,200-ton iron-hulled Victorian battleship, a monster with a ram bow, hit *Victory* below the waterline. Perhaps luckily for *Victory*, though suffering serious damage in the way of a 6ft x 2ft gash in her thick hull, *Neptune* had only been under tow to a German breaker's yard. *Victory* was quickly docked, spending several months having new timbers fitted before being spruced up and floated out in time for the Trafalgar centenary of 1905. In 1910, the distinguished maritime artist William Lionel Wyllie was asked to take the chair of the newly-formed Society for Nautical Research (SNR), an organisation dedicated to encouraging interest in matters relating to seafaring, shipbuilding and other nautical subjects.

The SNR set up a committee for the restoration of Nelson's flagship to her 1805 configuration, but everything ground to a halt on the outbreak of another war in 1914. Finally, after the war, the Society's president Admiral the Marquis of Milford Haven, was able to publish a groundbreaking report at the Annual General Meeting in June 1921, and additionally laid it before their Lordships of the Board of Admiralty, who approved his proposals. The Victory's future was secured. In December of the same year, the ship slipped her harbour moorings for the last time and was moved gently into No 1 basin at Portsmouth Dockyard, where work began on preparing her for permanent dry-docking.

The work of the SNR was crucial to the success of

Victory remained afloat at her moorings for a hundred years, her topsides slowly rotting from the ingress of rainwater. The ugly round bow fitted after Trafalgar, seen here in an early twentieth-century photograph, was the first item for replacement on the agenda of the Society for Nautical Research.

Victory's preservation as a permanent exhibit, for while the Board of Admiralty agreed to keep the ship on the Navy List, it could not fund the restoration of any part of the ship or its artefacts not strictly required to meet its function as a serving shore-based establishment, which is effectively what the ship would become once she was finally dry-docked. The SNR therefore launched a public appeal, *The Save the Victory Fund*, with a target of £50,000 which it hoped would be sufficient to start the ball rolling.

At the 1922 annual general meeting of the SNR, Admiral of the Fleet Sir Doveton Sturdee agreed the executive officers of the society should be the advisory experts as restoration of the *Victory* to her 'Trafalgar Condition' proceeded. However, it was also accepted that her condition could not be absolutely as it had been at the battle. By 1923, the fund stood at £30,000 and seemed to have come to a standstill. But then an anonymous donation of £50,000 enabled the real work to start. It was later discovered a Dundee shipowner, Sir James Caird, had made this extraordinary contribution to the fund. As *Victory* had moved into No 1 Basin in December 1921, work began almost immediately to prepare her for permanent dry-docking. This involved removing tons of ballast, artefacts and stores no longer required and this had the benefit of reducing strain on her elderly structure. Dry-docking any ship is always a delicate operation,

but in the case of *Victory*, particularly so.

It was known that her keel was distorted and more than 100 years afloat in Portsmouth harbour had caused some hogging of the hull, opening scarphs on the keelson by more than an inch. When, in 1922, an order was issued by the Admiralty Board for the ship to be preserved in No 2 Dock, a steel cradle was designed and built to give the waterlogged hull additional support. Once settled onto blocks in the bottom of the dock, and without the comforting and all-supporting fluid envelope, there was no telling what further distortion the massive wooden structure would suffer. Without the cradle, *Victory* might have distorted to the point of total collapse. While the technical aspects of a successful docking were obviously uppermost in the minds of all concerned with the project, the executive officers of the advisory restoration committee were also concerned with the aesthetics of presentation. The height of the docking blocks at high water spring tides – the highest tides of each equinox – were such that when all the water was drained from around her, Nelson's flagship sat low in the dock in, as the committee members put it, 'unspectacular' fashion. They pressed for the ship to be raised and were aided and abetted in this regard by the opinion of King George V when he visited *Victory* in July 1922. In the end best practice was relied upon; a procedure

that was thoroughly known to them and for which the tools, men and materials were readily to hand. To raise the ship the required amount involved carrying out the operation three times, using divers on each occasion to raise the blocks, then pump out the dock and secure the ship before starting the process all over again. To overcome excessive strain the rig would impart to the hull of the ship while land-locked in her new elevated position, holes were bored through the bottom of *Victory*; her masts being stepped on an arrangement of steel pillars and plates cemented into the dock bottom to support the hundreds of tons of spars and miles of rigging above. From an engineering point of view, the task was made easier by the fact that at some time in the 1880s, probably during a dry-docking in 1887, *Victory's* original wooden lower masts were replaced by the hollow wrought-iron masts of the 1870s frigate *Shah*. As a further precaution to secure the whole mass of rigging, extra stays were attached to each of *Victory's* masts and embedded at the sides of the dry-dock, effectively removing the major rig stress to *terra firma*.

THE GREAT SURVIVOR

The chronological list of repairs and refits to HMS *Victory* since 1812 is a long one. Once she was dry-docked, it was one of the first tasks of the 1920s

A watercolour sketch of *Victory* by William Lionel Wyllie showing reconstruction work in progress replacing the round bow with the original beakhead. Wyllie used this and other sketches when painting his famous oil, *Victory in the Pink. (Private collection)*

View of *Victory* through the attic window of buildings opposite No 2 Dock.

programme to reinstate the original beakhead bow and to replace the dilapidated upper deck with teak. It was also apparent much of the vessel's topside planking needed immediate replacement. Other than regular upkeep maintenance, painting and cleaning, no major repairs were undertaken for some time after 1928. The first refit had already cost the SNR £107,000 and it would not be too long before it was discovered that much of the work carried out in the first six-year programme would have to be repaired again at a later date. During the Second World War, a German bomb hit the masonry steps of the dock wall, tearing an 8ft by 15ft hole in *Victory's* port side, but she survived the blitz of Portsmouth otherwise unharmed. However, a far more lethal enemy lurked within her. The death watch beetle was discovered eating its way through some of the massive timbers of *Victory* in 1932, yet it was not until 1954 that the entire ship was first fumigated. Two more fumigations followed in the same decade but it did not entirely rid the ship of the problem. But with the help of the Building Research

Establishment, the application of new types of paste insecticides and continued monitoring, the death watch beetle problem gradually receded... but it has not been eradicated altogether. Since the Great Repair began in the 1950s, it has taken more than forty years to complete all of the major structural works and eighty-eight years since the programme of restoration commenced in 1922. As with any ship entirely made of timber, material deterioration begins from the date at which the keel is laid. Had *Victory* not been Nelson's flagship, she would have gone the way of the majority of vessels of the Napoleonic Wars, working out a naturally useful lifespan, undergoing the normal programmes of repair to battle and other damage as required to keep her in service. Ultimately, it was the fact that *Victory* was a heroic admiral's flagship that saw her continuing in service long after all the others in the fleet had gone to the breaker's. Without *Victory's* connections to Nelson and Trafalgar, we would not be able to visit this amazing vessel in the twenty-first century.

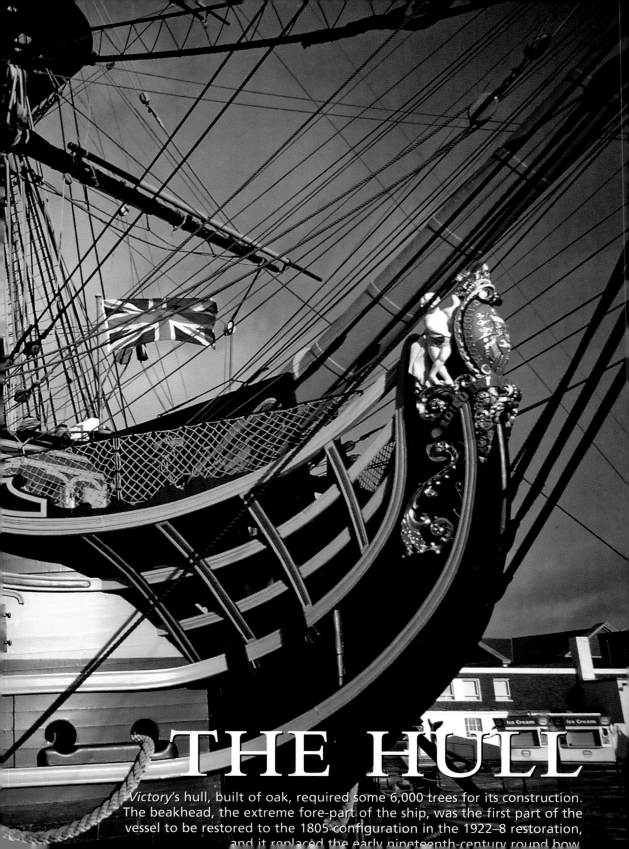

THE HULL

Victory's hull, built of oak, required some 6,000 trees for its construction. The beakhead, the extreme fore-part of the ship, was the first part of the vessel to be restored to the 1805 configuration in the 1922–8 restoration, and it replaced the early nineteenth-century round bow

AS FIRST NAVAL LORD BETWEEN 1830 AND 1834,
Victory's former Captain, Thomas Hardy, rescinded an
order to scrap the ship after his wife persuaded him to
tear it up. The Admiralty procrastinated for many more
decades, finally issuing a preservation order in March
1922; she was then moved to dry dock for restoration
and preservation.

Sir Thomas Slade's design for *Victory* was evolu-
tionary rather than radical. As First Rates of the era go,
Victory's underwater lines displayed a relatively fine and
rounded entry *(left and right)*, balanced to provide
excellent buoyancy forward.

Victory could spread a maximum of thirty-seven
sails, a total sail area of 6,510 square yards
(5,468.4 sq m) and with a steady breeze one or two
points aft of the beam she could surge along at a
respectable 8½ to 9 knots. In a 30–40 knot blow, she
could get up to 10 or 11 knots with every stitch of
canvas set. During the chase across the Atlantic to the
West Indies in 1805, Nelson, desperate to catch his
foe, would have had the *Victory*'s Sailing Master drive
her as hard as sea and wind conditions would allow for
the safety of the ship.

Bottom, far left: English elm was used for the ship's keel, a
tight-grained timber favoured for its in-water stability and
ability to hold fastenings. A grown piece scarphed onto the
fore end of the keel shown here is riddled with copper sheet
tack holes along its outer edge. A section of the keel damaged
during the Second World War was replaced with teak.

Bottom left: A bomb dropped during a March 1941 enemy
air-raid narrowly missed the flagship, exploding on masonry
steps in the dock wall and causing considerable damage to the
ship's cradle and concrete plinth built to support the keel. The
blast tore an 8 x 15ft (2.4 x 4.6m) hole in the hull planking
and supporting timbers as well as a 5ft (1.5m) hole in the
orlop deck. Electronic sensors (two white boxes in the picture),
help monitor *Victory*'s hull movement.

Right: *Victory*'s massive weight, no longer supported by water,
is carried on a concrete block along the length of her keel and
by a series of steel supports at the turn of her bilge.

Opposite page: Looking up at the galleries from the bottom of the dock. The gudgeons, the ironwork attached to the hull with rings into which the pintles – pins on the rudder – are slotted to attach the rudder to the hull, are clearly visible. Just above the waterline are the emergency chains which could be used to control the rudder if the steering gear was damaged; they also prevented its loss should the gudgeons and pintles break.

Above: The steel cradle built to support the hull. Both the colossal lateral and downward forces have to be counterbalanced.

Left: In March 1780 the bottom of the ship below the waterline was sheathed with 3,923 sheets of copper to protect her hull against the ship worm. Each copper plate measured 4ft x 14ins (1.22m x 35.6cm). These copper sheets and the nails would have weighed in the region of 15 tons. All of it has gradually been stripped from the hull, but vestiges of it remain on the huge rudder. Also visible is the ironwork for the gudgeons and pintles.

Victory's hull at the waterline is approximately 2ft (0.6m) thick, and she displaces a massive 3,500 tons. Almost all the oak for her construction was sourced from the forests of England and the Baltic. Elm and pine was also used, in total, an equivalent area of nearly 100 acres of woodland.

Left: Thirty-five years after her launch at Chatham, *Victory* underwent a substantial rebuild in the years 1800–03. Sir Thomas Slade's original open stern galleries were closed with windows and shutters. The rows from top to bottom are the Captain's and Admiral's cabins and officer's wardroom. Ships' names first appeared on the sterns of Royal Navy ships in 1778.

Right: The starboard lantern. Each lantern was supported by a bracket attached to the poop.

Bottom left: Third Rate ships and larger had three octagonal lanterns fitted on the taffrail at the stern. When lit at night they helped the ship astern to keep her station in the line of ships. The largest, in the centre, would signify the Flagship, the Admiral's ship.

Bottom right: Lead flashing at the top of the quarter galleries, as found in ordinary homes ashore, keeps the rainwater out.

Above: The starboard quarter galleries. Open quarter galleries were introduced in the sixteenth century for use as latrines. By the 1770s they were mainly closed in as are these on *Victory*, but their function remained the same. Quarter galleries, protruding as they do from the main structure of the ship, were relatively lightly built so as not to put too much strain on the after timbers.

Port quarter galleries viewed from quarterdeck level *(above)* and from below *(left)*. The boom of the fore and aft mizzen mainsail extends far out over the ship's stern.

HMS *VICTORY*
Dimensions and Tonnage

Length overall – end of bowsprit to taffrail:
226ft (69m)

Length of gundeck – roughly equivalent to the modern measurement of length between perpendiculars: **186ft** (56.6m)

Length of keel for tonnage – a rather arcane figure used for working out tonnage; not the actual length of the keel: **151ft 3⅜in** (59m)

Breadth – the broadest part of the midship section:
51ft 10in (15.7m)

Depth in hold – roughly the height of the ship's usable interior space: **21ft 6in** (7m)

Tonnage, burthen – a measure of burthen, ie carrying capacity in the hold; from a formula which was divided by 94, which explains fractions in ninety-fourths:
2,162²²⁄₉₄ tons (no metric equivalent)

Tonnage, displacement – the actual weight or displacement of water: **3,500 tons** (3,556 tonnes)

SHIP'S CARVING

Left: The figurehead and trailboards of *Victory*. Figureheads had become a firm feature of English ships by the mid seventeenth century and during that era were extravagantly designed and decorated. By the end of the eighteenth century they had become more modest affairs, partly to offset the cost of the wars with France.

Victory's figurehead is a replica of the Hanoverian royal arms, supported by two cherubs and mounted on the beakhead of the ship. This is the figurehead from the time of the battle of Trafalgar which replaced the more elaborate original carving during the great repair of 1801–03. A small scale replica of the original can be seen in the Royal Naval Museum, Portsmouth.

Right: *Victory*'s gilded main entrance on the starboard side. Entry ports were introduced into high-sided three-deckers because the distance from the waterline to the gunwale was too far to climb easily and they were mainly used by captains, admirals and official visitors. Others would have used the steps and lifelines to the right to clamber up and over the gunwale from launches when the ship was at sea. The single arch form with the decorated brackets at the side was typical of the late eighteenth century.

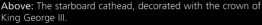
Above: The starboard cathead, decorated with the crown of King George III.

Main picture: The effect of extreme tumblehome to topsides created a large gap between the upper decks when similar ships came together and made it difficult to board the enemy. At the battle of Trafalgar this reverse curve of the hull prevented men of *Victory* easily boarding the French *Redoutable*, and vice versa. Tumblehome also increased stability as the weight of the ship was moved down towards the waterline.

Top right: One of twelve 12pdr guns on the quarterdeck, the smallest gun on the ship.

Centre: The sick bay window on the middle deck.

Bottom: The smaller hinged openings in the gunports were used for lighting, observation and musket sniping.

Below: The lower deck, just above the waterline, was the widest part of the ship and carried the heaviest guns.

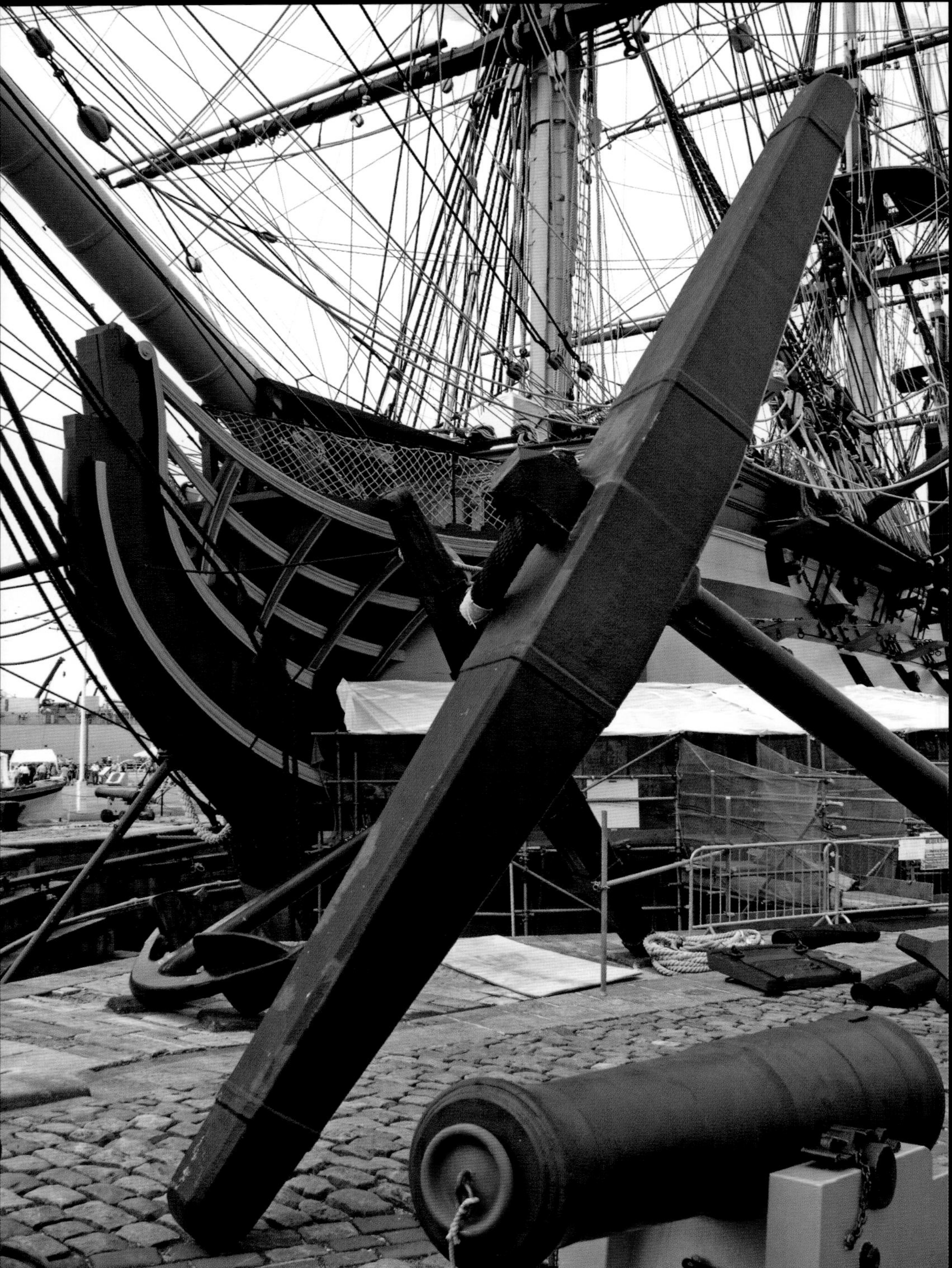

ANCHORS

Anchors were essential to the safety of vessels driven by the vagaries of wind. *Victory* and other large ships-of-the-line carried four main bower anchors deployed in readiness, attached to substantial rope warps up to 120 fathoms (720ft/219m) in length. Three smaller anchors were also carried. The process of heaving a laid anchor back aboard required the involvement of most of a ship's crew split into various teams to man the capstans, secure the weighed anchor stock to the cathead and 'fish' its flukes.

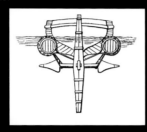

Right: The smallest anchors, kedge anchors, were small enough to be taken out by boat. They could be slung under a ship's launch and rowed to a position ahead of a ship in light weather or in confined anchorages before being dropped.

Left: One of *Victory*'s four huge bower anchors (which held the ship by her bows, hence the name), each weighing between 4 and 4½ tons, laid out ashore. The stock, shown here, is made of two pieces of oak.

Top right: In a rolling seaway, the spear-like flukes of huge anchors could damage a ship's planking as the anchor was weighed; it was important to get them secured, 'fished', as soon as possible.

Right: The cathead had to be particularly strong and fine-grained timber and projected from the top of the round of the bow to port and starboard of the hull topsides. At this time the support knee, designed to distribute the weight of the anchor, converged with the head rail. Used for stowing the anchor, it is fitted with rope sheaves, eye bolts, thumb cleats and a slip. *Victory*'s starboard cathead was shot away during the battle of Trafalgar.

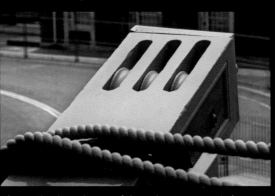

Above: The three sheaves of the cathead were made from lignum vitae and were positioned in the slots a little off centre, towards the ship, to help prevent the catfalls from jamming.

THE
LOWER DECK

Looking forward along the length of *Victory*'s mostly original port lower gundeck with massed ranks of 32pdr guns. A passing sailor uses a torch in the dim light, not much brighter than in 1805.

LAUNCHED AT CHATHAM DOCKYARD 7TH. MAY 1765.

EXTREME LENGTH 226' 6"   LENGTH OF KEEL 151' 3"
EXTREME BEAM 52' 0"   DEPTH OF HOLD 21' 6"
LENGTH OF GUN DECK 186'   TONNAGE 2162 TONS. DISPLACEMENT TONNAGE 3500TONS

ARMAMENT.

LOWER DECK 32 PDR, MIDDLE DECK 24 PDR, MAIN DECK 32 LONG 12 PDR, UPPER DECK 12 SHORT 12 PDR.

The greater part of the lower deck planking is thought to be original. It was the main living quarters for many of *Victory*'s crew. Hundreds slept and took their meals here and shared the space with the 32pdr guns which on the port, or larboard, side, are exhibited ready for action without the mess tables in place. This was also the deck where the anchor cable entered the ship and when the ship was at anchor the cable was made fast round the massive riding bitts, above left.

Left: The illustrated builder's board on the lower deck. These decorative boards were made by shipwrights in the dockyards where ships were built.

CAPSTANS

Capstans were powerful mechanical instruments used mainly for hauling anchor hawsers, though they were also used for lifting the ship's boats and any other heavy gear like masts and spars.

Victory had two double capstans located on the lower and middle decks, the main capstan and the jeer capstan forward of the mainmast. The upper and lower drums could be used independently or, by means of locking pins, together. A continuous 16in (40.6cm) diameter messenger turned around the lower drum and ran around posts forward on the lower deck enabling efficient cable handling.

Right: The lower deck capstan drum, parts of which may pre-date Trafalgar. A maximum of ten men per capstan bar could be deployed, thus 260 men altogether on the upper and lower capstans.

Below: A small part of one of *Victory*'s three 24in anchor cables secured on bitts at the forward end of the lower deck. The weight of cable helped significantly to keep a ship anchored on station and in the case of *Victory*, each of her three 120-fathom (720ft/219m) cables weighed 7 tons.

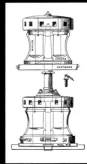

Above: The drawing shows how the oak whelps, attached to the central spindle, added diameter and thus increased the gearing of the capstan.

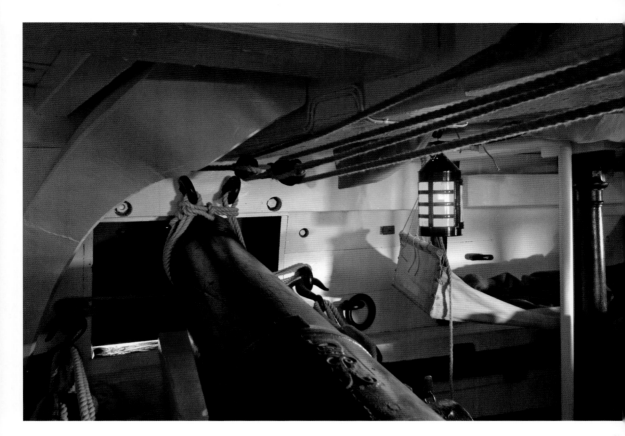

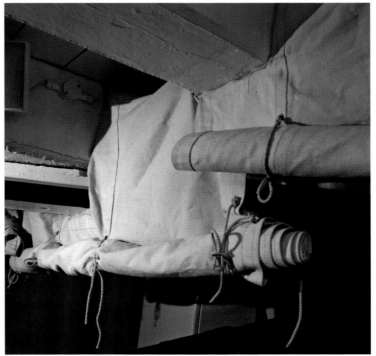

Above: *Victory's* gunner, chaplain and junior officers lived at the after end of the ship on this deck. Gunner William Rivers' hammock cot can be seen, right, next to the 32pdr. A canvas screen separated the gunroom from the rest of the deck and this and the hammocks would have been cleared away for action stations. When at sea the gun muzzles were lashed to prevent the guns lurching across the decks.

Right: For Jack Tar, there was little or no privacy onboard. Warrant officers, however, had designated spaces, or 'cabins', separated from the hurly-burly of shipboard life on the lower decks by canvas screens like these.

Right: By the mainmast two chain pumps worked from the lower gun deck pumped out bilge water accumulated from leaks, the ingress of rain or as a result of hull damage. With 150 men operating the cranks *Victory'* pumps could lift 120 tons of water per hour overboard. Separate elm pumps could also be used for washing down the decks and for fire-fighting.

Below: Ships' tillers of this period were made of oak or ash, the latter being preferred for its flexibility. Wooden tillers were always square in cross section. *Victory's* wooden tiller replaced an iron tiller that had probably been installed in the 1824 repair, and it is positioned close under the gunroom deckhead. Lieutenant John Quilliam led a team of sailors to the lower deck and jury-rigged the huge 29ft (8.8m) tiller enabling *Victory* to continue manoeuvring after her wheel was shot away early during the battle of Trafalgar.

Right: The square plates with their edges, or fiddles, spawned two common phrases in the English language: 'A square meal' and 'on the fiddle', the latter deriving its meaning from the food touching the fiddle, suggesting a large portion which had perhaps been acquired inappropriately.

GUNS

At the battle of Trafalgar *Victory* carried the following armament, a total of 104 guns. Apart for the two massive carronades, the heaviest guns, the 32pdrs, were located on the lower deck to assist stability.

Lower Gun Deck: 30 x 32pdrs
Middle Gun Deck: 28 x 24pdrs
Upper Gun Deck: 30 x 12pdr (long)
Quarter Gun Deck: 12 x 12pdr (short)
Forecastle: 2 x 12pdr (medium),
2 x 68pdr carronade

Below: The truck carriage carrying the gun was the standard means of mounting a gun throughout the age of sail. It was robustly built and carried a lot of strain. The recoil was brought up short by the breechings (the heavy ropes in the photograph) but nonetheless injured many men in battle. The recoil also put severe stress on the timbers of the ship. Each 32pdr gun required tackles and other equipment for the gunners *(see pages 88-89)*.

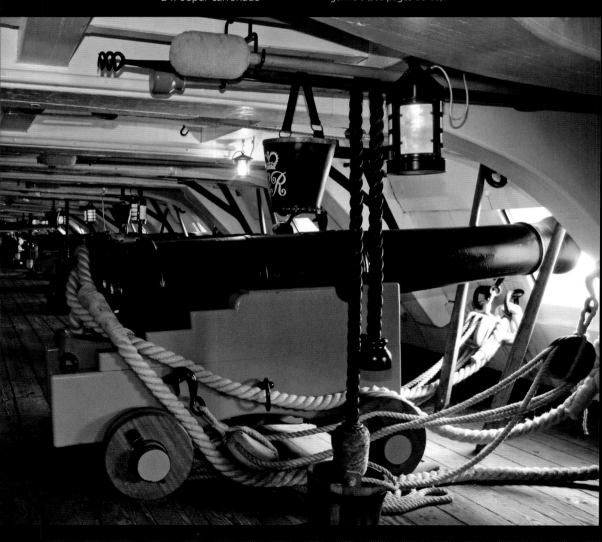

Top right. One of the carronades on the forecastle. This lumpy weapon was only 5ft 4ins (1.6m) long. It weighed 36 cwt (1.8 tons) but packed a considerable punch.

Whereas a 32pdr 'long gun' had an effective range of several hundred yards, or more when its ball could be 'skipped' by an expert gunner, the carronade was a short-range 'smasher'. Invented in 1752 by the Carron Ironworks of Scotland and manufactured from about 1778, it came into British naval service in 1780 in 12pdr, 24pdr and 32pdr versions. HMS *Victory* carried two large 68pdr carronades on port and starboard sides of her forecastle.

Right: The Thomas Blomefeld 32pdr gun. This beast measured 9ft 6ins (2.85m) overall and weighed almost 61 hundred-weight, a little over 3 tons. Some 32pdrs were slightly longer to increase their range to 2,640yds (2,402m). *Victory*'s Gunner William Rivers (1755–1817) calculated one man was needed for every 5cwt (272kg) of gun weight to operate it efficiently, thus in this case, a crew of twelve.

By the second half of the eighteenth century the 32pdr was recognised as the ideal weapon for the ship of the line and the heaviest that could be efficiently operated on a ship.

Below: The dockside cannon display.

THE ORLOP DECK AND HOLD

The orlop deck provided the space for stores that needed to be accessible, like the carpenter's store shown here. Out of picture to the left it stored, floor to deckhead racks of timber. Being below the waterline this deck was relatively safe in battle, so here also were located the surgeon's operating space and two powder magazines.

When the ship was in action the open after cockpit on the orlop deck *(top right)* was taken over and used as an operating theatre for the surgeon. One of the most common operations the surgeon would perform was amputation, using the instruments displayed on the right hand side of the lower photograph.

It was here that physician Sir William Beatty (1770–1842) and his team of medics attended the wounded during the battle of Trafalgar. Having been mortally wounded Nelson refused to be carried here, knowing there was no surgery that could save him. It was on this deck that he died and his name is inscribed on *Victory's* Roll of Honour Board *(top left)* displayed there.

The surgeon's cabin was on the orlop, right aft on the starboard side, and beside it was the dispensary *(above left)*. This was a lockable storeroom where the surgeon could safely store his drugs, powders and ointments.

The orlop was a dark and gloomy place, with little light filtering down through the stairwells or the gratings and lanterns provided the main light. Even the seat of ease (the heads) which were lit by a small porthole required the additional light of a lantern *(far right)*.

The midshipmen slung their hammocks in the cockpit *(top left)* and had a little more space and privacy than the ordinary seaman. The bosun's cabin *(lower left)*, though furnished with only the bare essentials, was better still with its fixed bunk. Just forward of the cockpit was the sail room where spare sails were kept and, on either side, the cable tier, a slatted floor where the anchor cable could drain down into the hold.

Another officer who inhabited this deck was the Purser, who needed to be close to the provisions and stores. Astern on the port side was the purser's slop room *(above)*. From here the purser sold clothes and bedding to the seamen as it was needed, and also tobacco.

Left: There were two hanging magazines on the orlop deck. The grand magazine, forward in the hold below, was the main gunpowder storage and charge making area, holding up to 35 tons (35.7 tonnes), of which 7½ tons (7.65 tonnes) were expended at Trafalgar. The walls of this and the two smaller hanging magazines are lined with copper. The metal reduced the possibility of sparks, kept the powder dry and prevented rats spreading powder around the ship. Once charges were made up they were stored in three different areas: in the grand magazine filling room and in two hanging magazines on the orlop deck.

Right: The small entrance to one of the hanging magazines, lined with copper sheet. The small white frame gives access to the racks of charges stacked inside and was more easily navigated by a powder monkey than a grown man.

Above left: Right aft was the steward's room. The ship's steward was the Purser's chief assistant and responsible for issuing the daily rations of food and drink to the mess cooks. The steward also slept here as a security measure to stop the theft of stores and was the most junior member of the ship's complement to have a fixed and private berth. The large bins were used for short-term storage.

Top: Narrow passages, or wing passages, between the inner hull and bulkheads of the cabins and store spaces enabled the ship's carpenter to inspect the ship's hull structure below the waterline and make any repairs without having to move stores.

Above: Timbers and inner planking of the transom, parts of which are thought to be original. This space housed the breadroom.

Left: *Victory* followed Vice Admiral Cuthbert Collingwood's 100-gun *Royal Sovereign* into action around midday on 21 October. Within an hour, the bulk of the British fleet were engaged in what Nelson described to his flag-captain, Captain Thomas Masterman Hardy, as 'warm work', a ferocious battle fought at close range, often with ships engaging more than one enemy simultaneously. A little after 1pm, Nelson was shot by a sniper positioned in the mizzen top of the French *Redoutable*; a single muzzle shot pierced his left shoulder, travelling downward through his torso, severing the pulmonary artery in the process. He was carried off the quarterdeck down to the orlop where the ship's surgeon Beatty was already frantically trying to save the lives of many mutilated in the battle raging noisily above.

Nelson was laid to rest here. Some say, as the depiction of the scene in the large oil painting by Arthur William Devis (1763–1822) suggests, against one of the ship's massive wooden knees. In more recent years, evidence, or the lack of it, indicates Nelson was laid flat on the deck in this location, possibly the only clear space to be found in the unfolding chaos of the moment. He died several hours later, at about 4.30pm.

Beatty had Nelson's body immersed in brandy and spirits of wine for the long voyage home in a barrel like the one below.

Overleaf: The bosun's store carried everything the ship would have needed in the way of rope and cordage.

The hold was used for long-term storage and for heavy spare items of ship's equipment. It was also where the grand magazine and the pump well were located.

Left: Looking forward into the massive hold space where up to six months worth of food and drink could be stored mostly in barrels embedded in shingle to stop them from moving around when the ship was at sea. The largest barrels, or leaguers, holding 150 gallons (682.5 litres) of water, were topped by smaller barrels filled with salted beef and pork, peas, sugar, vinegar and wine and 50 tons of beer.

Top: A sailor surveys the massive timbers used in the restoration of the flagship's lower bow section at the forward end of the hold. The whole bow structure was restored between 1980 and 1989.

Above: At the base of the mainmast, two pumps fashioned from the trunks of elm trees supplied approximately 25 gallons (113 litres) of seawater per minute for washing down decks and firefighting. One pump discharged onto the lower gun deck, the second onto the upper gun deck.

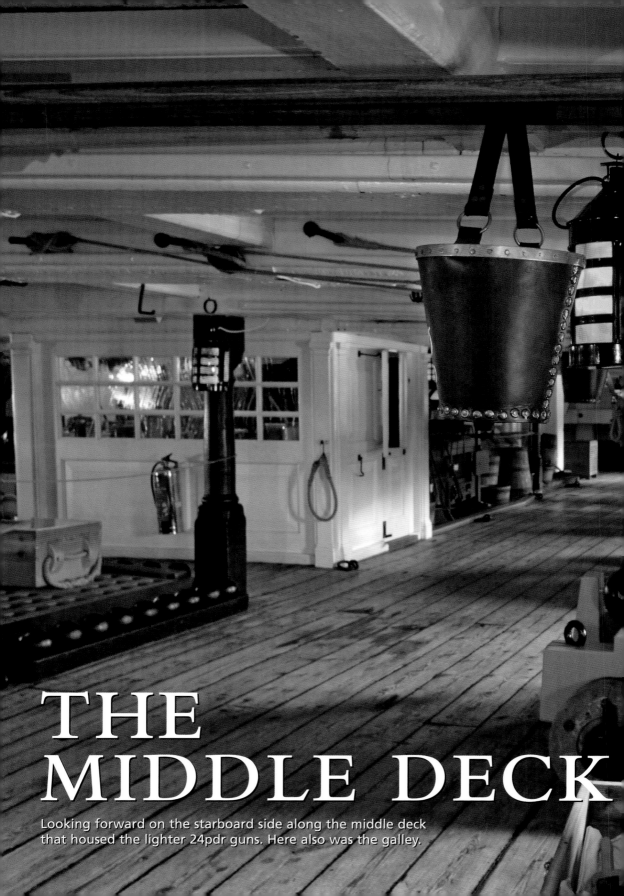

THE
MIDDLE DECK

Looking forward on the starboard side along the middle deck
that housed the lighter 24pdr guns. Here also was the galley.

On a fighting ship the middle deck was first and foremost a gun deck. Most of the 800 crew that manned *Victory* lived and ate between the guns, and slept in hammocks slung on battens between the deck beams. The sides of the ship were painted with a lime-wash that enhanced the light and helped to eliminate bacteria.

Above: Cook's barrels of foodstuffs mingle with shot charges around the foremast. Note the large wedges used to keep the mast tight where it passes through the deck.

Top right: Every man was given a hammock, a wool mattress and two blankets.

Right: In inclement and cold weather, the detachment of Marines enjoyed the warmest situation aboard ship, opposite the Brodie stove, here on the middle deck.

FEEDING
THE NAVY

The galley produced the food for all the ship's crew; it was the only galley onboard and catered for officers and men. The floor space was paved with bricks or flagstones as a precaution against fire. Food was cooked on a cast-iron Brodie stove, patented by a Scot, Alexander Brodie, and used in the Navy from 1781 to 1810. Two ovens produced up to 80lbs (36kg) of bread while two copper boilers made 250 gallons (1,137 litres) of stew. The stove also has a grill and an automated spit for roasting meat. A copper distiller made 2 gallons (9.10 litres) of fresh water a day. The stove could be fired with coal, of which *Victory* carried some 50 tons, and also burned wood.

A SAILOR'S DIET

Breakfast: Burgoo – an oatmeal porridge
Lunch: Salted beef or pork, sometimes with pease – dried peas
Supper: Leftover lunch or cheese with ship's biscuit – the victualling yard in Deptford made 25,000 pounds of biscuit a day for the Navy
8 pints of beer or 2 pints of wine, and half a pint of rum

Above and right: The Brodie stove had a spit at the front driven by the chain on the left. By the open front of the stove there were facilities for both standing and hanging cooking pots. The ship's cook was usually a pensioner of the Greenwich Hospital, after an order of 1704 stated that precedence be given to 'cripples and maimed persons'.

Right: The pantry beside the stove was where food was prepared. The large wooden paddle by the open door was used to feed dough into and extract the cooked bread from the ovens. Rats were the perennial pests onboard ship.

Left: A view of the Brodie stove showing the condenser for distilling fresh water on top. The large tubs were for steeping the salt beef and pork.

ARMADA	1588	SOLE BAY	1672
DOVER	1652	SCHOONEVELD	1673
PORTLAND	1653	TEXEL	1673
GABBARD	1653	BARFLEUR	1673
SCHEVENINGEN	1653	USHANT	1692
FOUR DAYS BATTLE	1666	ST. VINCENT	1781
ORFORDNESS	1666	TRAFALGAR	1797
			1805

Left A mess table. The crew was divided into messes of four or eight men for meals. Each man took a turn to be mess cook preparing food, collecting it from the galley and serving it. Some ate from tables slung from the deck head while others used collapsible tables. Benches were placed on both sides. The larger container on the table would have been used to bring the crew's provisions to the table.

Far left: The uniform of a Marine. One hundred and forty-six Royal Marines commanded by a Captain of Marines were billeted on the middle gun deck. Four marine officers shared the wardroom with the naval officers while NCOs and Marines lived between the 24pdr guns.

Bottom left: Battle honours of the current *Victory* and her predecessors.

Above: The upper capstan drum located on the middle deck.

Below: A Cruikshank cartoon of sailors relaxing at their mess table on a Saturday night. (© *National Maritime Museum, Greenwich*)

IN THE HEAT OF BATTLE

Massive guns could carve a path of devastation from one end of an enemy ship to another. The French *Redoutable*'s crew stood little chance against the sustained rapid firepower of *Victory*'s guns as crews worked incessantly to pummel the enemy into submission. A properly trained gun crew could sustain a rate of six seconds per shot when using the gun lock working within very tight confines of the restricted space between guns. The cacophony of noise, vibration, smoke, sweat, fatigue and semi-darkness was immense and often lasted for hours on end.

Left: The cannon displayed onboard *Victory* are replicas made of glass-reinforced plastic. Guns supplied by the Ordnance Board while the ship was in service would have been rotated for repairs and maintenance.

Far left: Ships' gun carriages are made from more than thirty different wood and metal components, the brackets, transoms and trucks being traditionally made from elm while the sides and axle trees are of oak. *(Richard Eastland)*

Bottom left: When gun ports were closed, visibility inside the ship was very poor and not much improved when they were open.

Below: A painting by Caroline Beaumont depicts a gun crew in the heat of battle.

Below: When the battle of Trafalgar was over, *Spartiate*'s Captain, Sir Francis Laforey, logged the damage; 'The Foremast and Bowsprit badly wounded in two places. 1 shot well thro' the heel of Maintopmast, which splintered it much Fore & Main Shrouds shot away and several of the Top mast Do. Backstays running rigging all cut very much and several shots in our hull & several small grape shot in the Fore and Main masts.' The sample displayed on *Victory* is a modern but real example of damage caused by iron roundshot.

Bottom: All cannon were supplied to ships by the Ordnance Board and solid cast from iron or gun metal and differentiated by their weight of shot.

A gunner's view towards the enemy.

Right: The brass foot plate at the starboard side main entrance.

Below: Hammocks were slung on both sides of the deck allowing 14in (35cm) between each. When not in use they were stowed in hammock nettings on the poop and quarterdeck.

Left: Hammocks are secured to wood battens fastened on the face of deck beams.

Below: The elaborate decorative work on the ship's bell rope. The bell, rung every half hour during the watches, meant that the sailors were constantly aware of the time.

GUN TACKLE & EQUIPMENT

ackles were required to both move and restrain the
uns, while any amount of equipment was needed to
ad, train, fire and clean them.

r left: A black-powder horn was inserted into the touch
ole of the breech of the gun and powder poured in.The
ptain of the gun also had a priming wire with which to
erce the cartridge which helped the ignition of the charge.

eft: Cartridges, roundshot in ready-use racks, wads and a
ucket containing slow matches.
   Before the introduction of gunlocks the charge was ignited
ing the matches.

elow left: The gun tackles were used for moving the gun
ut through the port prior to firing, while the heavy
reechings, threaded through a ring on the cascable,
strained the distance of the recoil. A train tackle led to the
ntreline of the ship (not shown here) and prevented a gun
nning out when a vessel was heeled.
   The gunners' equipment included (from left to right) a mop
r barrel cleaning, rammer to ram in the gun barrel the
rtridge, the ball and a wad. Other items required for
perating the gun included a worm for extracting debris and
isfired ordnance, and a flexible rammer or mob.

elow: For safety, touch holes were covered by a lead sheet
hen guns were not in use.

Above: Gun crews used a handspike lever to adjust the
aim of a gun – heavy work at the height of battle.
Wedges, known as quoins, were used to alter elevation.

Below: A gunlock, a larger version of the device used to
fire a flintlock pistol, fitted to one of *Victory*'s 32pdrs.
Invented by Captain Sir Charles Douglas, it helped gun
crews maintain a rapid fire rate in battle. A lanyard
released the hammer, enabling the gun captain to stand
well clear of the gun's recoil.

Bottom right: Coils of hemp for the slow match kept close
to guns in netting slung between deck supporting columns.

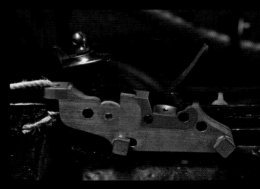

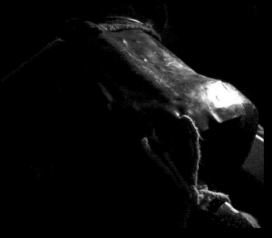

THE UPPER DECK

The upper deck mounted thirty 12pdr guns. As well as housing the admirals' quarters aft, it was also a working deck where the sailmaker and the carpenter, for instance, could carry out repairs.

Previous page: Admiral Nelson slept in a swinging cot between guns on the upper deck on the starboard side. The embroidered drapes are replicas of ones made for him by Emma Hamilton and now in the National Maritime Museum, Greenwich.

Above: A table in *Victory*'s Great Cabin with navigational instruments similar to the ones used on the ship in 1805; sextant (centre), dividers (bottom) and parallel rule (right) with charts showing the Straits of Gibraltar and southern Spain.

Far right: Admiral's quarters – a view looking aft from the starboard side, across the huge officers' dining table through to the Great Cabin right aft. Portraits of Emma Hamilton and Nelson and his decorated frock coat *(right)* are on display. The deck is covered with painted canvas. When the ship was cleared for action all the furniture and finery was taken away and stowed beneath the waterline.

Lower right: Grappling irons with ropes attached. These were stored on the upper deck so that they were accessible when needed on the quarterdeck.

GUNPORTS

Gunports were introduced around 1500 and they made possible the development of the heavily gunned warship. The port itself was cut between two frames and the gunport lid added to keep out water from the lower decks, make the decks more habitable against wet and cold and, lastly, help protect the gunners.

Right: Port lids were opened and closed from inside the ship using lanyard tackles. By the eighteenth century two tackles were used and two lines passed through the hull and then attached to eyebolts fitted at the bottom of the hinges. The ports could be quickly slammed shut by their own weight once the tackle was released.

Bottom left, opposite: Eyebolts were fitted on the inside of the lids so that they could be fastened shut.

Middle right: The port lid tackle under the deckhead used to haul open the lid. There was no leverage on a closed port so a bar was used to ease open the port lid a little before the tackle became effective.

Bottom right: Looking down on a raised lid. The long arms of the two hinges extended down almost the whole outside of the lid and added strength to the multi-timbered construction.

Below: The gunports of *Victory* on the lower, middle and upper decks. The lower deck ports, being close to the waterline, were kept shut except when the ship was in action.

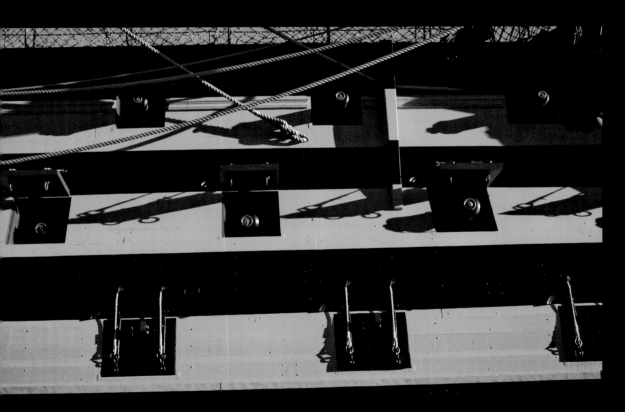

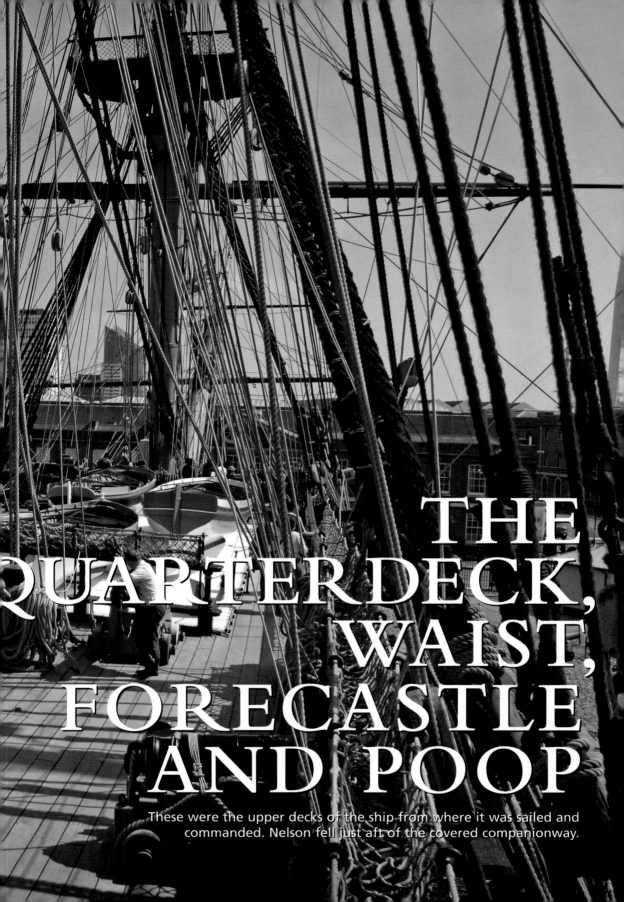

THE QUARTERDECK, WAIST, FORECASTLE AND POOP

These were the upper decks of the ship from where it was sailed and commanded. Nelson fell just aft of the covered companionway.

The double wheel controlled the tiller down on the lower deck. In a lot of wind and a heavy seaway, the strength of up to eight men was often needed to keep the ship on course. In fair weather the normal compliment for manning the wheel was four.

Sailors at the wheel concentrated on steering the course they were given, not by looking out or ahead, but by the compass. The compass rose was divided into 32 points and these defined the courses. The rose showed the four cardinal points, north, south, east and west; then the four half cardinals, NE, SE, SW and NW; the eight 'false' points as they were known, NNE, ENE etc; and finally the 16 points that divided all these, for example NbyE, NEbyE. Reciting the 32 points of the compass in order was known as 'boxing the compass'.

Left: The ship's wheel, protected by the overhanging poop.

Below left: *Victory's* wheel and binnacle. An endless rope turned around the drum of the wheel is connected to the rudder tiller on the lower deck. The wheel was destroyed during the battle of Trafalgar. The binnacle houses the ship's two compasses and a lantern for illumination at night.

Below: A halyard pin rail on the starboard side of the quarterdeck.

SHIP'S BOATS

Ships had boats of varying size used in all weathers for transporting dignitaries, officers, men, anchors, guns, stores and water butts around the fleet and to and from shore. It was in just such a 23ft-long cutter Captain Bligh was cast adrift in the Pacific Ocean after the mutiny on HMS *Bounty* and in which he and eighteen survivors voyaged an epic 3,618 miles (5,822km) to the safety of Coupang Bay. Toward the end of *Victory*'s time in the Baltic, small boats like this one were sent out to hunt down privateers.

Right: Another view showing the fine entry of a 25ft cutter. Smaller boats were used in all but the most inclement weather conditions and were easily and smartly handled under sail. *Victory* would have had six boats: a 34ft launch, a 32ft barge, a 28ft pinnace, and three cutters. The length of cutters varied and the two recently-built ones are 25ft. Cutters were usually clinker-built (the strakes of the hull overlapping and each fastened to ones adjacent) while the larger boats were carvel-built (the planks set edge to edge and fastened to frames).

Below: Looking forward over the waist where four of *Victory*'s boats could be stowed. The waist is now covered but once it would have been open and men made their way from the quarterdeck to the forecastle along the gangways (narrow decks either side of the waist). In the foreground is one of the cutters with her buff-painted interior.

Right: Four boats were stowed on skid cradles in *Victory*'s waist. Two more were slung from davits at the port and starboard quarters or secured by lashings at the chainwales. To the right of the Admiral's barge is *Victory*'s 34ft launch.

Above: An engraving by F Findon after a painting by E W Cooke entitled *Men-O-War at Spithead*. It shows a typical 74-gun ship preparing to weigh anchor, the commander and officers arriving by launch with a pilot boat nearby.

Above: One of *Victory*'s rowing and sailing cutters in the lowered position on the starboard quarter. Captive rowlocks for the oars are visible cut in the gunwale plank.

Opposite page: The mainmast just aft of the waist that has boarding pikes handily arrayed at the base. These were used by the Marines, and others, when boarding enemy vessels.

Left: The spot on *Victory's* quarterdeck where Nelson fell at about 1.15pm on 21 October 1805, marked by a wreath laid on Trafalgar Day 2004.

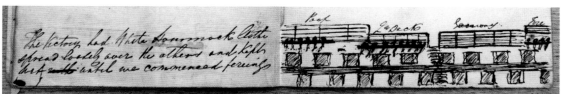

Above: A sketch from the notebooks of Richard F Roberts, a midshipman on *Victory* who was wounded at the battle of Trafalgar, showing the arrangement of hammocks packed in the netting along the sides of the poop and the quarterdeck. He describes how Marines were kept hidden on *Victory's* poop, quarter and foredeck using 'white hammock cloth' until firing commenced at the battle of Trafalgar. The stuffed hammocks also increased protection against small arms fire and were usefully stowed out of the way when they were not in use.

Right: The netting for the hammocks and the crutch-shaped iron stanchions, mounted on the port rail of the poop deck. The rings by which the netting was held and the bar across the top are clearly visible. The hammocks were kept dry with tarpaulins.

Opposite page: The poop deck provided an elevated position and this is the view the officers of the watch would have had looking forward. At anchor the Union flag is flown from the jackstaff positioned on the bowsprit. The forward end of the poop provided shelter over the wheel and binnacle. At the aft end of the poop was the signal locker where the signal flags were kept.

Above: The mizzen jeer and topsail bitts. The cross beam connecting the bitts has belaying pins for halyards and other items of running rigging. Jeer and topsail bitts are also located at the base of the mainmast and foremast.

Below: Leather fire buckets emblazoned with the insignia of King George III line the forward end of the poop beneath the hammock netting.

Above: The belfry bell was the ship's clock, the number of strokes telling the crew of the ship the time of day. It was rung every half-hour over a four-hour period – the length of a watch. At the end of a watch, the bell was rung eight times and then the same schedule restarted for the next watch.

FLAGS & SIGNALS

The use of the White Ensign *(opposite)* to differentiate today's Royal Navy ships from merchant vessels evolved from a time far back in English history when the Cinque Ports of Hastings, Winchelsea, Rye, Romney, Hythe, Dover, and Sandwich were incorporated by Edward the Confessor and required to furnish a naval fleet commanded by the Lord Warden.

Fleets were distributed into three squadrons: the Van, Centre and Rear, the rank of the commanding officer of each distinguished by a square flag of red, white, or blue respectively and worn at the main masthead. Nelson's flag was white, denoted in his title, Horatio, Viscount Nelson, Vice Admiral of the White.

The first White Ensign incorporating the St George's cross appeared in the sixteenth century. In 1707 the Union Flag appeared in the canton. In 1864 an Admiralty order reserved the White Ensign for its own use and other establishments such as The Royal Yacht Squadron. Under some circumstances, the Royal Navy may still use the Red and Blue Ensigns.

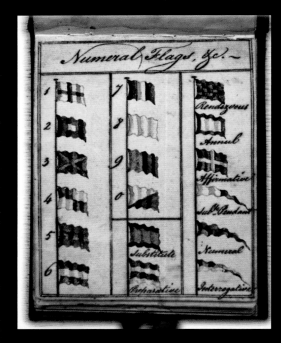

Above: Another page from Richard F Roberts' pocket notebook with superbly drawn coloured signal flags. Daytime communication between ships, and between ships and the shore, was by means of these signalling flags. The flag code used by ships at Trafalgar was developed by Admiral Home and was known as the Popham code. The code books contained some 6,000 words and useful short phrases.

Right: The Chief Quartermaster of *Victory* hoists part of Nelson's most famous signal to the British fleet before the battle of Trafalgar on the morning of the battle's 199th anniversary.

Above: HMS *Victory* is the Royal Navy's oldest ship still in commission, the flagship of the Second Sea Lord, and she is required to fly the White Ensign from her flagstaff.

Right: A White Ensign flutters from the stern of a modern British warship. Only the American destroyer USS *Winston S. Churchill* is permitted to fly the flag alongside her own national 'Stars and Stripes'.

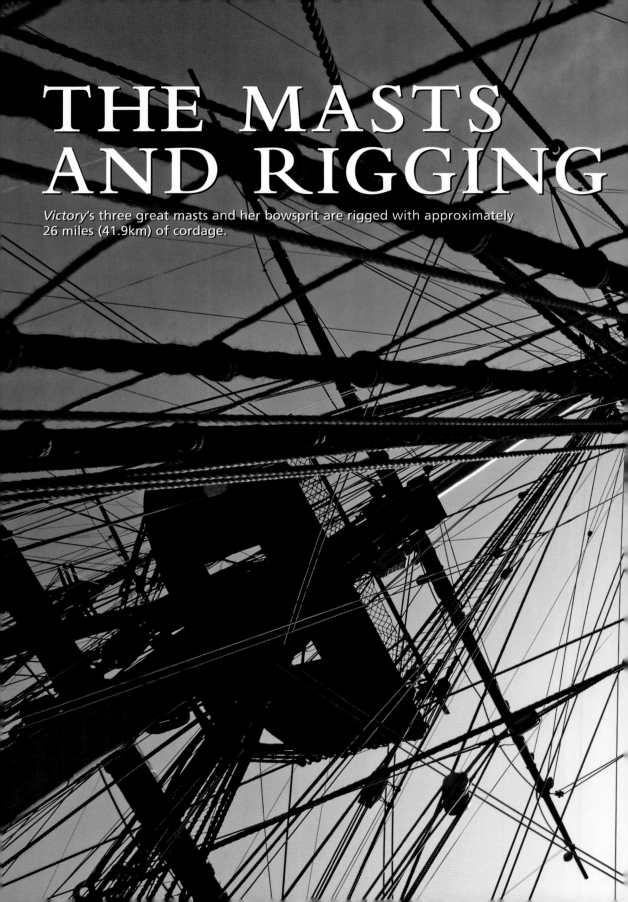

THE MASTS AND RIGGING

Victory's three great masts and her bowsprit are rigged with approximately 26 miles (41.9km) of cordage.

Above: The fighting tops are the platforms at the top of lower sections of *Victory*'s masts from where Marines poured musket fire into ranks of enemy sailors and soldiers below, a practice frowned upon by Nelson. It was the same practice that resulted in Nelson being shot by a soldier of the French 16th Infantry Regiment, Robert Guillemard, who had been ordered into the mizzen top of the 74-gun *Redoutable*.

Left: Parrel beads were strung on any rope that kept a yard attached to a mast. The small wooden balls reduced friction and facilitated easy movement.

Above: The ratlines were, effectively, a rope ladder made of well-stretched light cordage secured across the mast shrouds at 15in (38cm) intervals enabling sailors to climb aloft to the tops and sail yards.

Top: Where an eye was needed in large ropes, the practice of worming and serving locked the tail securely to the standing part. Blacking down the rigging helped preserve it and involved rubbing a mixture of vegetable and mineral tar into ropes on a warm day.

Main photo: The mainmast stay and preventer stay, part of the ship's standing rigging. All masts required stays (running forward), backstays (running aft) and shrouds (side stays) to keep them in place. A simple but effective arrangement of lanyards and pendants rove through wooden thimbles allowed adjustments to be made as required.

On the three yards were set, from the lower one, the main course, the main topsail and the main topgallant.

Inset: The main preventer stay, an additional stay supporting another when that one is subject to great strain, is made fast to the foremast using thimbles and a lashing.

Without blocks and pulleys, it would be almost impossible to manoeuvre or sail a large ship, let alone work the guns. Some 1,400 elm or ash blocks are used for the rigging and guns aboard *Victory*.

In the seventeenth and eighteenth centuries a whole industry was dedicated to block manufacture. One of the largest suppliers to the Admiralty was the Southampton firm Taylors, founded by Walter Taylor in 1754, who realised many accidents at sea were caused by poorly-made blocks and pulleys.

After trials of a new type of block in HMS *Centaur*, Taylors were ordered by the Admiralty to supply blocks and pulleys for each ship in the Navy, followed by a replenishment order in 1779 when the entire stock of spares at Portsmouth was destroyed by fire.

At the peak of supply, Taylors averaged 100,000 blocks a year but their contracts were cancelled in 1803 after the invention of a revolutionary steam driven block milling machine by French émigré Marc Isambard Brunel. Ironically, Brunel's machines, erected in his Blockmills in Portsmouth Dockyard, reached their production peak at about the time of the outbreak of the Crimean War, a point in maritime history marking the demise of sail and the beginning of steam-powered ships.

Deadeyes are stout discs of wood pierced through with three holes or eyes and because they are not fitted with pulleys they are said to be 'dead', thus 'deadeyes'. The holes enable purchase lanyards to be set up and tensioned on the lower ends of mast shrouds and secured to chainplates fixed below the chainwhale (a horizontal wooden platform) to the hull; 216 deadeyes are used on the standing rigging.

Left, top and bottom: The two main treble jeer blocks and the two main double jeer blocks by which the massive main yard was hoisted.

Below: A single block on the outside of *Victory*'s hull.

Above: Five of the starboard side foremast shrouds. Beneath the lower deadeyes are the chainplates that are fastened to the ship's side.

Right: The port mizzen deadeyes, upper and lower, which, with their lanyards, support six shrouds. The chainwhale, visible at the bottom, kept the chains and lanyards away from the sides of the ship and also increased leverage.

Below: Three upper deadeyes. The lanyard was first attached to the deadeye using a stopper knot. After being rove through the holes of the deadeyes it was fastened around the bottom of the shroud.

Below: *Victory's* bowsprit, with its jibboom and flying jibboom beyond, is 110ft (33.5m) long and is the spar (or mast) upon which the ship's triangular fore sails and two square spritsails were set. The two yards for the spritsails are clearly visible. They were only set in the lightest winds; in any sort of breeze they tended to bury the bow down. In the foreground, left, is the thimble and lanyard for the foremast stay.

Just below this, out of picture, is the 'Marines' Walk', or gangboard, a wooden grating giving access to the bowsprit from the forecastle. An armed Royal Marine sentry patrolled the gangboard when the ship was anchored to stop crew members deserting over the ship's bow.

Right: *Victory's* bowsprit seen from below. The bowsprit cap (into which the jibboon fitted) and the dolphin striker can be seen at the top of the photograph. Just as the bowsprit was held down by the bobstay leading to the stem of the ship, so the jibboom was supported by stays leading to the lower end of the dolphin striker.

Left: Restoration and conservation are ongoing. An expert from Bell Rigging carries out a visual inspection on the mizzen mast just below the topgallant yard. Industrial Roped Access techniques based on those used in caving and mountaineering are used in this dangerous work. *(Photo Aneurin Cooper)*

Above: A conservator with the Mary Rose Trust demonstrates a special vacuum cleaner used to clean one of ninety shot holes in *Victory's* 200-year-old fore topsail that survives from the battle of Trafalgar. The enormous sail has now been surface cleaned using these low-powered vacuum suction brushes and statically-charged cloths.

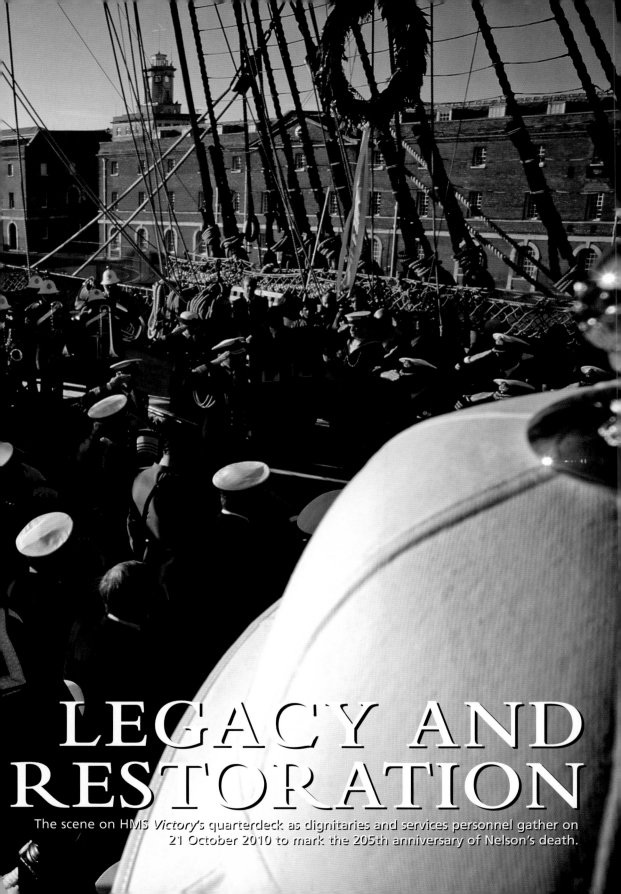

LEGACY AND RESTORATION

The scene on HMS *Victory*'s quarterdeck as dignitaries and services personnel gather on 21 October 2010 to mark the 205th anniversary of Nelson's death.

Left: A Union flag flown by HMS *Spartiate* at the battle of Trafalgar is one of the few complete flags remaining from that day. *Victory*'s ensign draped Nelson's coffin but was purloined by sailors during the funeral service at St Paul's Cathedral and torn into small pieces. A sample is framed behind glass on the ship's orlop deck.

This flag was presented by *Spartiate*'s crew to its First Lieutenant, James Clephan (1768–1851) for outstanding courage during the battle. The ship first engaged the *Formidable* and was then in a running battle with five other ships before turning her attention to the 80-gun Spanish *Neptuno*. After an hour of pummelling, the Spaniard struck.

The *Spartiate* was a 1,949-ton, 74-gun Third Rate ship-of-the-line built by the French at Toulon in 1794 and named *La Spartiate*. She was captured by Nelson at the battle of the Nile. *(Photo Charles Miller © Charles Miller Ltd.)*

Above: Nelson's tomb at St Paul's Cathedral, London.

Right: Vice-Admiral Lord Nelson, played by Alex Naylor.

Opposite: The 17ft (5.2m) figure of Nelson sculpted in Craigleith stone by Edward Hodges Baily surveys the Nation's capital from atop a 169ft 3in (51.59m) granite column in Trafalgar Square, seen and remembered by thousands each day. *(Jonathan Eastland by kind permission of the National Gallery)*

Far left, top: The ribbon of a wreath hoisted above the spot on *Victory*'s quarterdeck where Nelson was felled by a French sniper's musket ball, swirls in a gentle autumn breeze, a moving reminder of the great commander's spiritual presence long after his demise.

Far left, bottom: 1930s gold plate and enamelled tea caddy spoon emblazoned with an image of HMS *Victory* is typical of artefacts sold or given away since the ship was opened to the public. Hundreds of thousands of similar ornamental objects, cigarette cards and cake tins can be found in homes throughout the United Kingdom.

Main photo: Descendants of those who fought at the battle of Trafalgar, including aboard HMS *Victory*, gather beside the ship in 2005.

Top: Sophisticated twenty-first-century radio-controlled models re-enact scenes from 200-year-old famous Napoleonic sea battles at a 'Meet Your Navy' display in Portsmouth's Historic Dockyard.

Below: Five-ton Turkish cannon cast in 1790–1 in the reign of the Ottoman Sultan Selim III, captured by Admiral Sir John Thomas Duckworth from the island of Kinaliada, Sea of Marmara, in 1807 and transported to England.

The cast-iron carriage featuring plaques commemorating British Naval victories at the battles of Nile and Trafalgar was made at the Royal Carriage Department of the Royal Arsenal, Woolwich.

The gun was displayed for several years at Devonport Naval Museum as seen here, before returning to the Old Royal Naval College, Greenwich, where it was first installed in 1807.

Almost from the moment her keel was laid in Chatham Dockyard in July 1759, *Victory* was bound to suffer the fate of all vessels built from wood, rope and canvas. Plagued by the vagaries of climate, of continual expansion and contraction and most notably, rot from the ingress of rainwater into her planks, and later timber-eating insects, the ship has been in a state of more or less continuous maintenance, repair and restoration for well over 250 years. It is often said in maritime circles, regarding wooden ships, once you have finished at one end, it is time to start again at the other.

Apart from wear and tear, the ship suffered considerable damage while on active service from enemy action and dire weather conditions experienced in the Baltic between 1808 and 1812. She was holed in a collision with HMS *Neptune* in 1903, and in the early 1970s fire crews struggled to put out a blaze deep in her bow section, started as paint was being stripped from old timbers.

Very little of the ship originally completed in 1765 remains; but this is not the point. Many ships undergo minor or major modifications for different reasons during their lifetime; what remains at the end may be something very different from what appeared at the beginning. In *Victory*'s case, it is to the dedication of the cause of keeping the ship in its Trafalgar state that the nation owes thanks to the 1922 members of the Society for Nautical Research and, subsequently, to the countless individuals who have contributed to her well being.

Below: The armed schooner HMS *Pickle* captained by Lieutenant John Richard Lapenotiere battled gales in the Bay of Biscay to bring news of the British victory and the death of Nelson at Trafalgar. Since then *Victory* and her admiral have attained iconic status. A replica of the vessel is seen here in 2005 moored in No 1 basin astern of *Victory*'s home in No 2 Dry Dock. The original *Pickle* was built in Bermuda of cedar and was one of many Admiralty off-the-shelf acquisitions. No plans of the vessel exist.

Left: *Victory's* figurehead and part of her beakhead undergoing restoration in 1983.

Right: Repairs in 1971. Work on fitting new frames and outer planking to the aft port side.

Below: Repairs to the bow structure were carried out between 1980 and 1989, the beakhead and new figurehead being unveiled in May 1990.

SOURCES

NATIONAL MUSEUM OF THE ROYAL NAVY

RNM 1998.41, A collection of three volumes relating to Gunner William Rivers and Lieutenant William Rivers and their service on board HMS *Victory*.

RNM 1994.128, Anonymous Account of the Battle of Trafalgar.

RNM 1983.1065.1 Small memorandum book of miscellaneous content kept by Midshipman Richard Roberts of HMS *Victory*, 1805.

RNM Research File, John Whick Royal Marine Musician, Letters from HMS *Victory* 1808 – 1812.

Information Sheet No. 9, Samuel Hood.

Information sheet No. 50, HMS *Victory* – a chronology.

Information Sheet No. 56, Augustus Keppel.

ROYAL MARINES MUSEUM

RMM 11/12/42 Letters of Lieutenant Lewis Roteley.

NATIONAL ARCHIVE

ADM 38/9286 and 38/9287, HMS *Victory*, Ship's Log.

OTHER SOURCES OF INFORMATION

Account of HMS *Victory*'s history published by H.M. Dockyard Chatham, 1965.

Some Notes on the Building of H.M.S. Victory at Chatham And the Dockyard at That Time, based on records at the NMM, Greenwich and the PRO. Compiled for H.M. Dockyard, Chatham, M.Y.T. September 1959.

SELECTED WEB SITES

www.hms-victory.com
www.flagship.org.uk
www.royalnavalmuseum.org
www.nmm.ac.uk
www.ageofnelson.org
www.jmr.nmm.ac.uk
www.paintedships.com/lossvictory.asp

PUBLISHED SOURCES

Adkins, Roy, *Trafalgar, The Biography of a Battle* (Little, Brown, 2004).

Ballantyne, Iain, *H.M.S. London* (Pen & Sword, 2003).

————, and Eastland, Jonathan, *H.M.S. Victory* (Pen & Sword, 2005).

Beatty, William, *The Authentic Narrative of the Death of Lord Nelson* (London, 1807).

Bryant, Arthur, *Nelson* (Fontana Books, 1972).

Callender, Geoffrey, *The Story of H.M.S. Victory* (Philip Alan, 1929).

————, *Sea Kings of Britain, Vol. 3,* (Longmans, 1939).

Clarke, John D, *The Men of HMS* Victory *at Trafalgar* (Vintage Naval Library, 1999).

Clowes, William Laird, *The Royal Navy, A History From the Earliest Times to 1900*, Vols 2–5 (Chatham Publishing, 1996).

Davies, David, *Fighting Ships* (Robinson, 2002).

Fenwick, Kenneth, *H.M.S. Victory* (Cassell, 1959).

Fremont-Barnes, Gregory, *The Royal Navy 1793–1815* (Osprey Publishing, 2007).

Gardiner, Robert (ed), *Nelson Against Napoleon* (Chatham Publishing, 1997).

————, *The Campaign of Trafalgar 1803–1805* (Chatham Publishing, 1997).

————, *The Line of Battle* (Conway Maritime Press, 2004).

————, *Fleet Battle and Blockade* (Chatham Publishing, 1996).

Goodwin, Peter, *Nelson's Victory* (Conway, 2004).

————, *The Construction and Fitting of Sailing Men of War 1650-1850* (Conway Maritime Press, 1987)

Hattendorf, John B, Knight, R J B, Pearsall, A W H, Rodger, N A M, and Till, Geoffrey (eds), *British Naval Documents 1204–1960* (Ashgate Publishing, Navy Records Society, 1993).

Hibbert, Christopher, *Nelson, A Personal History* (Penguin, 1995).

Jackson, T S (ed), *Logs of Great Sea Fights 1794–1805*, Vol 2 (Navy Records Society, 1900).

Kennedy, Ludovic, *Nelson and His Captains* (Fontana/Collins, 1976).

King, Cecil, *H.M.S. (His Majesty's Ships) And Their Forebears* (The Studio Publications, 1940).

Lambert, Andrew, *War at Sea in the Age of Sail* (Cassell, 2000).

Lavery, Brian, *Nelson's Fleet at Trafalgar* (National Maritime Museum, 2004).

————, *Life in Nelson's Navy* (Sutton Publishing, 2007).

————, *The Arming and Fitting of English Ships of War* (Conway Maritime Press, 1987)

Le Fevre, Peter, and Harding, Richard (eds), *Precursors of Nelson* (Chatham Publishing, 2000).

Lloyd, Christopher, *The Nation and the Navy* (Cresset Press, 1961).

Mackenzie, R H, *The Trafalgar Roll* (George Allen, 1913).

MacDonald, Janet, *Feeding Nelson's Navy* (Chatham Publishing, 2004)

May, W E, *The Boats of Men-of-War* (Chatham Publishing, 1999)

McGowan, Alan, *HMS Victory, Her Construction, Career and Restoration* (Chatham Publishing, 1999).